THE

MOSES
PAPERS

CREATION

JEFFREY JOHNSON

THE MOSES PAPERS

21st Century Press is a publisher dedicated to publishing books with high family values. We believe the vision for 21st Century Press is to provide families and individuals with user-friendly materials that will help them in their daily lives and experiences.

It is our hope that this book will help you discover truths for your own life and help you meet the needs of others. May you be richly blessed.

ISBN: 978-0-9894317-6-7

Cover Design: Lee Fredrickson
Book Design: Lee Fredrickson

21stCENTURY
P R E S S
READING YOU LOUD AND CLEAR.

DEDICATION

This study is dedicated to my two sons Stephen and Scott. Their lives inspire me to be a better man and to embrace life with a passion. The Moses Papers is about God's creation – that man is created in God's image and that God breathed into man the soul of life, thus having principle significance. Profoundly life is to be lived to the fullest in God. My sons reflect God's image in respecting, protecting, loving and cherishing life – I am a blessed man!

The soul, the breath of God,
came from God and through
faith in Jesus Christ it returns
to spend eternity with its
divine source.

You are different from the
beasts of the field by virtue of
your intellect, free will, self-
awareness, consciousness
of the existence of others,
conscience, responsibility and
self-control.

Being created 'in the image of
God' implies that human life
is infinitely precious.

CONTENTS

God says He will make a
way for you to move forward
in the wilderness you may
be experiencing and give you
water, and sustain you, in the
dry barren desert that has
overwhelmed you.

Using This Book:

Style

Lectures in Genesis is a verse-by-verse study of Genesis 1:1 – 2:7 highlighting the historical context, Rabbinical and Evangelical interpretations of the text, and unlocking the meanings of certain Hebrew words.

Format

Outline numbers and letters appear in the text that correlates with the numbers and letters of the "Student's Notes." This enables the student to follow the teacher in a more precise fashion.

Author

Dr. Jeffrey D. Johnson is a humanitarian, pastor, educator, guest speaker in conferences, colleges nationally & internationally (including Harvard), author, and president of Israel Today Ministries: www.israeltodayministries.org

It came to pass that, in a
certain finite time and in a
certain finite place, the infinite
God sent forth His *Memra* to
intersect the finite and to be
clothed in garments of human
flesh, "And the Word became
flesh" (John 1:14). So Miriam
(Mary), a daughter of the
house of Israel, "was found
to be with child by the Holy
Spirit" (Matt. 1:18)

INTRODUCTION

A KISS FROM GOD

*May he kiss me with the kisses of
his mouth (Song of Songs 1:2)!*

a. This is the cry of the bride – a desire for more of
    the Beloved, a desire for intimacy. The Shulamite
    maiden (Israel, the Bride of Messiah, the individual
    soul for whom Messiah died) is speaking here.
    She is not satisfied with relationship at a distance.
    She desires close contact. Kissing only occurs in
    close, face-to-face relationships.

b. The Scripture tells us that God spoke to Moses
    p'anim al p'anim, face to face suggesting intimacy
    (Exod. 33:11). He spoke to the people of Israel at
    various times and in different ways throughout the
    prophets. But in these last days, He has spoken to
    us by *His Son, Yeshua* (Hebrews 1:1, 2)[1].

c. What is a kiss from God? According to rabbinic
    tradition, it is when God kisses an individual
    through His Word:

Regarding Song of Solomon 1:2:

"An angel would carry forth the Word from before the Holy One, blessed be He, word by word, going about to every Israelite and saying to him, 'Do you accept upon yourself the authority of this Word?'... And the Israelite would say 'Yes.' Then he would kiss him on his mouth…It was the Word itself that make the rounds of the Israelites one by one, saying to each one, 'Do you accept me upon yourself?...And the Israelite would say 'yes.' …and the Word of God kisses the Israelite on the mouth." (Song of Songs Rabbah 2:2,1; Targum to the Song of Songs, Ch. 1, v. 2).

d. When you read the Bible and a verse suddenly becomes alive to you, an "aha!" moment, literally coming off the page to you, and you know that God is speaking to you – you have been kissed by God!

May God kiss you with a thousand kisses during our study of Genesis!

A. Title

1. Bereishit (Hebrew, בראשית)

    Book names in Hebrew are usually taken from the first or second word found in the book itself. *Bereishit* is the Hebrew name derived from the first word in the Bible meaning "in the beginning." Originally, call *Sepher Maaseh Bereishit*, meaning "The Book of the Act of In the Beginning" [2].

2. Geneseos (Greek)

    In the Greek translation of the Old Testament (Septuagint) the first book of the Bible is called *Geneseos,* which is the Greek translation for the

Hebrew word *toldot*, which is the English word *generations* [3]. The Greek name means "The Book of Origins."

3. Genesis (English)

Genesis comes from the Greek *geneseos* and also means "The Book of Origins."

B. Author

1. Moses wrote the Book of Genesis. He was not an eyewitness to the events written within the book – he was a researcher compiling oral and written traditions and in the end editor of the information. However, he was an eyewitness when writing Exodus, Leviticus, Numbers and Deuteronomy (with exception of his birth, death and subsequent events).

2. Genesis is a compilation of eleven histories (Hebrew Toldot). *Toldot* means generations, genealogy, or history of people or events – simply a family document.

3. Eleven Histories (Toldot, what became of, what happened?):

   1. Heavens and earth (2:4 – 4:26).
   2. Adam (5:1 – 6:8).
   3. Noah (6:9 – 9:29).
   4. Sons of Noah (10:1 – 11:9)
   5. Shem (11:10-26).
   6. Terah (11:27 – 25:11).
   7. Ishmael (25:12-18).
   8. Isaac (25:19 – 35:29).

      9. Esau, what became of Esau (36:1-8).
    10. Esau, what became of Esau as the father of the
        Edomites (36:9 – 37:1).
    11. Jacob (37:2 – 50:26).

4.   In the story of Creation the number seven occurs again and again.

5.   After the introductory verse (1:1), the section is divided into seven paragraphs, each of which appertains to one of the seven days.

6.   An obvious indication of this division is to be seen in the recurring sentence, *And there was evening and there was morning, such-and-such a day.* The Masoretes were right in placing an open paragraph (i.e. one that begins on a new line) after each of these verses[4].

7.   * First Paragraph: Story of the First Day (1:2-5).
    * Second Paragraph: Story of the Second Day (1:6-8).
    * Third Paragraph: Story of the Third Day (1:9-13).
    * Fourth Paragraph: Story of the Fourth Day (1:14-19).
    * Fifth Paragraph: Story of the Fifth Day (1:20-23).
    * Sixth Paragraph: Story of the Sixth Day (1:24-31).
    * Seventh Paragraph: Story of the Seventh Day (2:1-3).

8. Each of the three nouns that occur in the first verse – God (*Elohim*), Heavens (*samayim*), earth (*eretz*) express the basic concepts of the section (1:1 – 2:3) as they are repeated in a given number of times that is a multiple of seven:

9. *God* occurs thirty-five times, that is, five times seven.

10. *Heavens*, (firmament [*raqia*], expanse, sky, visible arch in the sky) appears twenty-one times – that is three times seven.

11. *Earth* (dry ground, land) is found twenty-one times.

12. There are ten sayings with which, according to the Talmud, the World, was created (Aboth v 1; in B. Rosh Hashana 32a).

13. These ten sayings are divided into two groups:

    Seven sayings regarding the creation of the creatures.

    · Let there be light (1:3)
    · Let there be a firmament, or expanse (1:6)
    · Let the waters be gathered together (1:9)
    · Let the earth put forth vegetation (1:12)
    · Let there be lights (1:14)
    · Let the waters bring forth swarms (1:20)
    · Let the earth bring forth (1:24)

    The second group emphasizes God's concern for man's welfare.

- Let us make man [not a command but an expression of the will to create man] (1:26)
- Be fruitful and multiply (1:28)
- Behold I have given unto you every plant yielding seed (1:29)

14. The terms *light* and *day* are found, in all, seven times in the first paragraph (2-5).

15. *Water* is mentioned seven times in paragraphs two and three (6-13).

16. *It was good* appears seven times (the seventh time - *very good*).

17. The first verse has seven words: (הַשָּׁמַיִם וְאֵת הָאָרֶץ בְּרֵאשִׁית בָּרָא אֱלֹהִים אֵת) *"Barasheet bara Elohim et hashamaim v'et haeretz"[In the Beginning God created the heavens and the earth].*

    These first seven words, in Hebrew, comprise a total of twenty-eight letters, or, four times seven.

18. The second verse contains fourteen words – twice seven.

19. To suppose that all this is a mere coincidence is not possible. This numerical symmetry is, as it were, the golden thread that binds together all the parts of the section[5]. Simply, there was a divine plan and purpose beyond human reason, or myth – there is a great designer behind the words.

20. That Moses wrote the first five books (Torah) is confirmed in Scripture: (Exod. 17:14; Lev. 1:1,2;

Num. 33:2; Deut. 1:1; Josh. 1:7; 1 Kings 2:3; 2 Kings 14:6; Ezra 6:18; Neh. 13:1; Dan. 9:11-13; Mal. 4:4; Matt. 8:4; Mark 12:26; Luke 16:29; John 7:19; Acts 26:22; Rom. 10:19; 1 Cor. 9:9; 2 Cor. 3:15).

C. Purpose of Genesis

1. The purpose of Genesis, which is part of the Torah (first five books of the Bible written by Moses), is to ascertain that God is the Sovereign of all Creation. *"He has made known to His people the power of His works, in giving them the heritage of the nations" (Psa. 111:6).*

2. Genesis (Torah) is a book of laws and is a record of the instruction given to man regarding his place and purpose in the universe.

3. When man failed God disciplined them, however he did not abandon them – he gave them a way to repent – he gave them a way to come back to God.

4. The patience and love of God is highlighted within the Books of Moses. Between Noah and Abraham is ten generations. Each generation failed in some way to obediently follow God. He then chose Abraham.

5. The Torah is a record of morality emphasizing our relationship to God and life's truths about personal growth, love, hate, pain, joy, tragedy, family, and hope.

D. Two Divisions[6]
Arnold Fruchtenbaum charts two divisions of Genesis:

	First Division	Second Division
Scripture	1:1 – 11:9	11:10 – 50:26
Subject	FOUR EVENTS: Creation 1:1 – 2:25	FOUR PEOPLE: Abraham 11:10 – 25:8
	The Fall 3:1 – 2:25	Isaac 25:9 – 26:35
	The Flood 6:1 – 9:29	Jacob 27:1 – 36:43
	The Nations 10:1 – 11:9	Joseph 37:1 – 50:26
Themes	Beginning of the Human Race	Beginning of Jewish People
	Origins of the World the Nations in General	
Style	Historical	Biographical/ Biographical History
Geography	Fertile Crescent from Eden to Haran	Canaan, Haran, Egypt
Time Period	2,000+ years	193 years

PREFACE

GENESIS 1:1-31 - 2:7 NASB

The Creation

¹ In the beginning God created the heavens and the earth. ² The earth was formless and void, and darkness was over the surface of the deep, and the Spirit of God was moving over the surface of the waters. ³ Then God said, "Let there be light;" and there was light. ⁴ God saw that the light was good; and God separated the light from the darkness. ⁵ God called the light day, and the darkness He called night. And there was evening and there was morning, one day.

⁶ Then God said, "Let there be an expanse in the midst of the waters, and let it separate the waters from the waters." ⁷ God made the expanse, and separated the waters which were below the expanse from the waters which were above the expanse; and it was so. ⁸ God called the expanse heaven. And there was evening and there was morning, a second day.

⁹ Then God said, "Let the waters below the heavens be gathered into one place, and let the dry land appear;" and it was so. ¹⁰ God called the dry land earth,

and the gathering of the waters He called seas; and God saw that it was good. [11] Then God said, "Let the earth sprout vegetation, plants yielding seed, and fruit trees on the earth bearing fruit after their kind with seed in them;" and it was so. [12] The earth brought forth vegetation, plants yielding seed after their kind, and trees bearing fruit with seed in them, after their kind; and God saw that it was good. [13] There was evening and there was morning, a third day.

[14] Then God said, "Let there be lights in the expanse of the heavens to separate the day from the night, and let them be for signs and for seasons and for days and years; [15] and let them be for lights in the expanse of the heavens to give light on the earth"; and it was so. [16] God made the two great lights, the greater light to govern the day, and the lesser light to govern the night; He made the stars also. [17] God placed them in the expanse of the heavens to give light on the earth, [18] and to govern the day and the night, and to separate the light from the darkness; and God saw that it was good. [19] There was evening and there was morning, a fourth day.

[20] Then God said, "Let the waters teem with swarms of living creatures, and let birds fly above the earth in the open expanse of the heavens." [21] God created the great sea monsters and every living creature that moves, with which the waters swarmed after their kind, and every winged bird after its kind; and God saw that it was good. [22] God blessed them, saying, "Be fruitful and multiply, and fill the waters in the seas, and let birds multiply on the earth." [23] There was evening and there was morning, a fifth day.

[24] Then God said, "Let the earth bring forth living

creatures after their kind: cattle and creeping things and beasts of the earth after their kind;" and it was so. [25] God made the beasts of the earth after their kind, and the cattle after their kind, and everything that creeps on the ground after its kind; and God saw that it was good.

[26] Then God said, "Let Us make man in Our image, according to Our likeness; and let them rule over the fish of the sea and over the birds of the sky and over the cattle and over all the earth, and over every creeping thing that creeps on the earth." [27] God created man in His own image, in the image of God He created him; male and female He created them. [28] God blessed them; and God said to them, "Be fruitful and multiply, and fill the earth, and subdue it; and rule over the fish of the sea and over the birds of the sky and over every living thing that moves on the earth." [29] Then God said, "Behold, I have given you every plant yielding seed that is on the surface of all the earth, and every tree which has fruit yielding seed; it shall be food for you; [30] and to every beast of the earth and to every bird of the sky and to every thing that moves on the earth which has life, I have given every green plant for food"; and it was so. [31] God saw all that He had made, and behold, it was very good. And there was evening and there was morning, the sixth day.

Chapter 2

The Creation of Man and Woman

[1]Thus the heavens and the earth were completed, and all their hosts. [2] By the seventh day God completed His work which He had done, and He rested on the

seventh day from all His work which He had done. [3] Then God blessed the seventh day and sanctified it, because in it He rested from all His work which God had created and made.

[4] This is the account of the heavens and the earth when they were created, in the day that the Lord God made earth and heaven. [5] Now no shrub of the field was yet in the earth, and no plant of the field had yet sprouted, for the Lord God had not sent rain upon the earth, and there was no man to cultivate the ground. [6] But a mist used to rise from the earth and water the whole surface of the ground. [7] Then the Lord God formed man of dust from the ground, and breathed into his nostrils the breath of life; and man became a living being.

FIRST WORDS: GENESIS 1:1-3

A. First Words (1:1)

1. The seven words *"Barasheet bara Elohim et hashamaim v'et haeretz"(In the Beginning God created the heavens and the earth)* provide the foundation for the entire Bible.

2. The first word *bereishit* in English is three words, "In the Beginning." The word itself does not tell us when the beginning was, simply that this was the beginning of the heavens and the earth.

3. It refers to the first phase of a process, a step, the beginning of the heavens and earth as it now exists.

4. The statement of John 1:1 chronologically precedes Genesis 1:1. While John 1:1 also states: *In the beginning*, he goes on to state: *In the beginning was the Word, and the Word was with God, and the Word was God.*

5. By means of this Word, the heavens and the earth were created (John 1:3). So both Genesis 1:1 and John 1:1 mention the phrase *In the beginning*. Genesis 1:1 does not, however, reveal when *the*

beginning was, but *In the beginning* of John 1:1 chronologically precedes the *In the beginning* of Genesis 1:1, because obviously the Messiah, the Logos, the Word, the Memra, preceded the creation of the heavens and the earth.[7]

6.   The first word of the Bible, (*bereishit*, "In the beginning") can be separated to form two words: (*bar/ber*) and (*asheet/eishit*).

7.   The word (*bar*) means "son" or "a son"; thus the term **bar** *mitzvah* (son of the commandment), or *Simon* **bar** *Jonah* (Simon son of Jonah).

8.   This word first appears in the Bible in Psalms 2:12 "Do homage to [or 'kiss'] the **Son**..."

9.   The second word (*asheet*) is a verb which means "I shall put/place/appoint," and first appears in Genesis 3:15 where God pronounced a curse upon the serpent:

"And **I will put** enmity between you and the woman..."

10.   Now if we reposition the definitions of these two Hebrew words, we arrive at the phrase "A Son I shall put/place/appoint."

11.   A better rendering might be, "A Son I shall establish."

12.   The introduction of only a slight separation between the second and third letters of the Bible provides us with this insight.

13. Maybe Paul had this in mind when he encouraged Timothy in "correctly cutting, or dividing the word."

14. The second word *bara* is a word that is used only of God and of the work that only God can do. It is never used with anything that man does.

15. It could mean to create out of nothing, but is also used to create out of something. For example, the universe was created out of nothing, but Adam and Eve were both created out of something.

16. When something is created, what is produced is new, fresh, and good.

17. The word carries the concept of shaping, forming, and transforming.

18. *Bara* is used in the creation of the heavens and earth, 1:1; Jehovah created the heavens, Isa. 42:5; created the host of Heaven, Isa. 40:26; Creator of the ends of the earth, Isa. 40:28; created the north and the south, Psa. 89:12.

19. Of the creation of living creatures – of animal life, 1:21; of human life, 1:27 5:1,2; 6:7, Deut. 4:32; Psa. 89:47; Isa. 45:12; of the cosmic forces of nature, Isa. 45:7; Amos 4:13; of Israel, Eccl. 12:1; Isa. 43:1; Isa. 43:7; Isa. 43:15; Mal. 2:10.

20. Of transformation and renewal of things – God creates a new thing in the earth, Num. 16:30; He creates a clean heart, Psa. 51:10; He creates

waters in the desert, Isa. 41:18-20; He creates salvation, Isa. 45:8; He creates peace, Isa. 57:19; the heavens and the earth, Isa. 65:17; Jerusalem, Isa. 65:18; a new thing, a woman (Israel, or virgin) shall encompass (surround/protect) a man, Jer. 31:22. (Israel will embrace Her God; and will cling to her Divine Husband).

21.   In Genesis 1:1 God called the universe into existence, and He created the universe *ex nihilo*, Latin for "out of nothing." This is verified by Romans 4:17, *God, who…calls the things that are not, as though they were*; and by Hebrews 11:3, *the worlds were framed by the word of God, so that what is seen has not been made out of things which appear.* As the Creator, He is the Creator of both the material and immaterial universe, and this is why there is something rather than nothing.[8]

22.   Verse one says nothing as to when the beginning was, just that this was the beginning of the heavens and the earth. It refers to a first phase of a step, the beginning of the universe as it now exists.

23.   To repeat what was stated earlier in paragraph numbers 4 & 5; the statement of John 1:1 chronologically precedes Genesis 1:1.

While John 1:1 also states: *In the beginning*, it goes on to state: *In the beginning was the Word, and the Word was with God, and the Word was God.*

24. By means of this *Word*, the heavens and the earth were created (John 1:3). So both Genesis 1:1 and John 1:1 mention the phrase *In the beginning.*

25. Genesis 1:1 does not reveal when *the beginning* was, but the *In the beginning* of John 1:1 chronologically precedes the *In the beginning* of Genesis 1:1, because obviously the *Messiah*, the *Logos*, the *Word*, the *Memra*, preceded the creation of the heavens and the earth.[9]

26. *Memra*: Then God said... The Torah depicts God creating the universe through the agency of speech. He speaks and there is.

27. In the days of the Apostles and for a few centuries thereafter, Aramaic paraphrases of the Torah (called *targums*) personified God's spoken word as a sort of temporal manifestation of God.

28. Jewish theologians of the day could not comprehend an infinite God intersecting with the finite – it was impossible within their thinking. How can an infinite God fit in the finite universe?

29. As a result they theologically conceived of an abstraction of the totality of God whereby God might interact within finite time and space.

30. They regarded this abstraction of God as a projection of the infinite into finite form, and it was termed "the Word."

31. The Aramaic term is *Memra* (מימרא), a word that

literally means, "word." Consider the following paraphrase of Genesis 1:1-3 from one such Aramaic *targum*:

> *From the beginning, with wisdom the Word* (מימרא, *Memra*) *of the LORD created and perfected the heavens and the earth...And the Word of the LORD said: "Let there be light"; and there was light by his Word. (Genesis 1:1-3 Targum Neofati Yerushalmi).*

32. The *targum* depicts the *Memra* as the active agent of God, ordering and creating the universe.

33. In the gospel of John, the *Memra* of God seems to be equivalent to the *Logos* of which John speaks (John 1:1-3). The word Logos also means "Word," and John's emphasis is that the Word is God and pre-existed before the creation, however, became flesh.

34. It came to pass that, in a certain finite time and in a certain finite place, the infinite God sent forth His *Memra* to intersect the finite and to be clothed in garments of human flesh, "And the Word became flesh" (John 1:14). So Miriam (Mary), a daughter of the house of Israel, "was found to be with child by the Holy Spirit" (Matt. 1:18).[10]

B. Regarding Regrets

O God, You Who are the truth, make me one with You in love everlasting. I am often wearied by the many things I hear and read, but in You is all that I long for. Let the learned be still, let all creatures be silent before You; You alone speak to me. – The Doctrine of Truth, The Imitation of Christ. Thomas A Kempis

1. Every time the scripture is read Jews believe they relive the Revelation at Mount Sinai, when their ancestors were silenced in awe at the foot of the trembling mountain, when they heard the thunder of God's voice.

2. It is so when we read God's word, we seek to come closer to the source and hear Him speak. We then desire and say, "Draw me, and we will run after You" (SOS 1:4 NKJV).

Divine Origin

1. The beautiful thing about scripture is that every word and every letter comes from Divine origin. What is the Divine origin? God.

2. Looking at the very first word of scripture we get a sound bite of God's provision and purpose for His pinnacle of Creation – people.

For the Sake of Torah and Israel

1. The first word is בראשית (*bereishit*, in the beginning, Genesis 1:1) is really two words. Rashi, a revered rabbinical scholar (1040-1145 AD) stated, the two words, Bar & Reishit (rasheet), means "for the sake of Torah/Israel. *Bar* means "son" and *Reishit* means "I will put" (Gen. 3:15). Jewish

scholars say that the "son" refers to Israel. Rashi added the idea "for the sake of Torah" – Torah referring specifically to the 5 books of Moses, generally referring to all of scripture, or the <u>Word</u> (of God).

A Son I Will Put

1. Simply, you can interpret *b'reishit* to mean "A Son (Bar) I will put (Rasheet)." Therefore, from the very beginning we have a reference to God's Son, an Anointed One that God will place, or appoint, or put. The Apostle John said it this way, "In the beginning was the <u>Word</u>, and the <u>Word</u> was with God, and the <u>Word</u> was God" (John 1:1 NKJV).

2. Jesus is the Torah/Word that was made flesh and dwelt among us (John 1:14). This gives great comfort to the fact that from the very beginning we learn of the Anointed One, the Messiah, the Lord Jesus.

Facing Forward

1. Let's take it one step beyond. The first letter of the first word is ב (the Hebrew letter "bet," בראשית (*bereishit*, in the beginning). The ancient sages suggest that, just as the letter *bet* is enclosed on three sides but open to the front (Hebrew is read from the right to the left), urges us to live our lives facing forward rather than looking backward.

2. *Bet* is the second letter of the Hebrew alphabet. The second letter emphasizes that even if we cannot begin at the very beginning, or undo, or revisit what is past, we are to move forward looking to hope, looking to God.

3. Are we to forget the past? Of course not – remember the blessings of God, "I will remember the works of the Lord; Surely I will remember Your wonders of old. I will also meditate on all Your work, and talk of Your deeds" (Psa. 77:11, 12 NKJV).

Regarding Regrets

1. However, regarding regrets, should of, would of, could of, we should look forward to God, and not worry what might have been, "Do not remember the former things, Nor consider the things of old. Behold, I will do a new thing, Now it shall spring forth; Shall you not know it? I will even make a road in the wilderness and rivers in the desert" (Isa. 43:18, 19 NKJV).

2. Here God says He will make a way for you to move forward in the wilderness you may be experiencing and give you water, and sustain you, in the dry barren desert that has overwhelmed you.

3. The first letter and the first word of the first book of scripture reminds us of hope and assurance of

the future as we move forward looking to God.

"Fear thou not; for I am with thee, be not dismayed; for I am thy God, I will strengthen thee; yea, I will help thee; yea, I will uphold thee with the right hand of my righteousness." (Isaiah 41:10 KJV)

C. Spirit of God (1:2)

1. A young Jewish carpenter stood up in the synagogue in Nazareth, stood up to read the Torah and the scroll of the prophet Isaiah was handed to him. He unrolled the scroll and began to read,

   'The Spirit of the Lord is upon me, because He anointed me to preach the gospel' (Lk. 4:18 NKJV; Isa. 61).

2. He looked at those in attendance that day and said,

   'Today this Scripture has been fulfilled in your hearing.' Doing this, He declared himself to be the Anointed One of God – the Messiah.

3. What was this Spirit? The same anointing Spirit is mentioned in Isaiah 11:1-2 – in fact the city of Nazareth was named after this passage, after "the Branch" (*Netzer* נצר) – which is a title for the Messiah. It is written, "He shall be called a Netzrin (Matt. 2:23)

4. Isaiah is telling us that the Messiah will come from the line of Jesse and that the Spirit of the Lord will rest upon him.

5. In the Midrash Rabbah (6th Century CE), an ancient collection of Jewish folklore and biblical commentary, states that this Spirit of the Lord that is spoken of in Isaiah that is resting upon the Messiah is the same Spirit of the Lord that moved over the primeval waters of Creation:

    "The Spirit of God was moving over the surface of the waters." This was the spirit of Messiah as it is written, "The Spirit of the Lord will rest on him (Genesis Rabbah 1:2)." [11]

6. To put Genesis in context we must go back to the Late Bronze Age, in the shadow of the majestic Pyramids, ancient science, magic and wonders, the children of Abraham encountered a world with many different interpretations on how the world and the universe began.

7. However, when you read the opening verses of Moses' Genesis you find a unique formula of communication. It is not a defense of a belief. It is not a political statement from a cult. It is simply a declarative piece of literature.

    "In the beginning God created the heavens and the earth" (Genesis 1:1).

8. Being divinely led by the Holy Spirit Moses opens the account with the Axiom, "In the beginning God created."

9. The declaration ends in Genesis 2:4, "These are the generations (report, description or history) of the heavens and of the earth when they were created..." Between these verses you discover the divine activities that unfolded.

D. Shekinah (1:3)

1. One of these divine activities is found in verse three where "light" is mentioned before the creation of the sun, moon and stars (Genesis 1:3-5; 14-16).

2. This is very peculiar. What was this light that existed before the sun, moon and the stars? Some theological sages say it was none other than God's glory that emanated throughout the universe or, God's Shekinah glory.

3. This essence was present throughout the wilderness wanderings and in the Tabernacle & Temple, as well on the Mount of Transfiguration the Shekinah was manifested in Jesus.

4. Furthermore, in the Book of Revelation we find that at the "end of time" the Shekinah will be present with the New Heaven and Earth, "And there shall be no night there; and they need no candle, neither light of the sun; for the Lord God giveth them light: and they shall reign for ever and ever" (Revelation 22:5 KJV).

5. Therefore, we have glimpse in understanding the eternal God. In the beginning, God was there.

In the end, God will still be there. His glory is brighter than any luminary. His presence is before all things and after all things. He is the absolute sovereign of the universe. Nature bows down before Him. He is not part of the natural world; rather, He is beyond its dominion.

6. So from the very beginning we have a declaration that God is, that He exists and is greater than all we see or understand. By His sovereign Will He created and spoke things into existence. The fact that He was before, and will remain after, is comforting.[12]

7. "And God said, Let there be light: and there was light" (Genesis 1:3).

    Light plays such an important role in the tradition of Judaism. Lighting candles on Shabbat (every Friday evening) is to remind Jewish people of their Creator and to sanctify this day from others.

8. Lighting the Hanukkah menorah is a memorial of the miracle of God's intervention on Israel's behalf in 168 B.C. also, the 7-branch menorah found in the synagogue and formerly in the Temple 'tells of an eternal light of divine origin, but tended by man.'[13]

9. They say this 'holy lamp bore light in the Temple and from there to the world.'[14]

10. Even the 'light' from Genesis 1:3, which was in existence before the luminaries (verses 14-19),

'was a light, according to the (rabbinical) sages, set aside for the future of Messianic fulfillment.'[15]

11. These beautiful symbols point to our Holy God in one fashion or another. Unfortunately, many Jewish people are blinded to the full meaning of the 'Light.' Paul stated, 'But even unto this day, when Moses is read, the veil is upon their heart' (2 Corinthians 3:15 KJV).

12. 'Light' in Scripture is usually synonymous with God, hope, the 'written Word' or the 'living Word' who is Jesus the Messiah.

13. For example, we find in the Gospel of Luke, as the angelic announcement came to the shepherds concerning Christ's birth, that 'the glory of the Lord shone round about them and they were sore afraid' (Luke 2:9).

     The 'glory' was this brilliant eternal light that terrified the shepherds as they realized they were in the presence of Holiness.

14. And, when Joseph and Mary entered the Temple with the child Jesus in order to fulfill the custom of the Law, (sacrifice for Mary's purification 40 days after the birth of a son), 'a just and devout' man took the baby up in his arms and stated that Jesus is 'A light to lighten the Gentiles, and the glory of thy people Israel' (Luke 2:32 KJV).

15. Jesus said in correlation to the significant emphasis on light, 'I am the light of the world: he

that followeth me shall not walk in darkness, but shall have the light of life' (John 8:12 KJV).

16. 'Darkness' describes the condition of man's heart. One will stumble in the darkness unless they have a light to guide their way.

17. Tradition, though beautiful, is not the 'light,' religion, though commendable, is not the 'light', self-esteem and self-awareness, though important, is not the 'light.' The Psalmist wrote, 'Thy word is a lamp unto my feet, and a light unto my path' (Psalm 119:105 KJV). He found the secret to 'dispel the darkness' namely, the Word of God.

18. The Apostle John stated, 'In the beginning was the Word, and the Word was with God, and the Word was God…And the Word was made flesh, and dwelt among us' (John 1:1,14 KJV).

19. Jesus, the Living Word, is the 'Light' that dispels the darkness of sin from your heart. He is the 'Passover Lamb,' the one without spot or blemish, the perfect sacrifice on Calvary for the sins of the world. You see, without shedding of blood there is no remission of sin (Hebrews 9:22). This is why the Cross.

20. Yeshua ha Meshiach, Jesus the Messiah, is 'the true Light, which lighteth every man that cometh into the world' (John 1:9 KJV).

21. The reason some (both Jew and Gentile) do not

come to the light is simply, as Augustine (354-430) stated in his first homily on the Gospel of John, 'there are insensitive hearts, still incapable of receiving this Light because the weight of their sins prevents them from seeing it. Let them not imagine that the Light is absent because they do not see it, for on account of their sins they are in darkness.' 'And the light shineth in darkness; and the darkness comprehended it not' (John 1:5). 'Therefore...like the blind man exposed to the sun, the sun being present to him but he being absent from the sun, so the insensitive one, the sinner, the impious has a blind heart.'[16]

22. Let us therefore examine our hearts to see if we are walking in the 'Light' or are walking in darkness. Do you know the Lord Jesus as your personal Savior or are you still walking in the darkness of your sin? The only light your neighbor may see is you. What do they see?

23. 'Ye are the light (reflecting the true Light) of the world. A city that is set on a hill cannot be hid. Neither do men light a candle, and put it under a bushel, but on a candlestick; and it giveth light unto all that are in the house. Let your light so shine before men, that they may see your good works, and glorify your Father which is in heaven' (Matthew 5:14-16 KJV)." [17]

24. Looking at the opening chapters of the book of Genesis we find the fundamental pillars upon which Judaism and Christianity rests.

25. Moses, directed by the Holy Spirit, writes this account of the creation of the universe and all living things. He does not describe the creation or birth of God as other contemporary cults of his time. Nor, does he try to validate any political or national ideals of the Hebrew people. Rather, he simply states that God is there, and that He spoke, and things were created.

26. He is the pre-existent God! Prior to creation there was nothing, except the Glory of God. God Himself, pre-existing before time itself, before anything existed, He was there.

27. Now this is hard for humans to comprehend. Before time existed, before there was anything, there was God in eternity past. In the Biblical account you will not find a physical connection, in terms of creation, between the human and divine. Simply, God spoke and it was done, "Let there be…" "For He spoke and it was done" (Psalm 33:9).

28. The phrase "in the beginning" is the Hebrew word, *Bereishit*. The rabbis conclude that since the first book of Moses opens with the second letter of the Hebrew alphabet, "bet" or "b," and that the Ten Commandments opens with, "I am the Lord your God," or the Hebrew word *anokhi,* thus beginning with the first Hebrew letter, "alef," or "a," that the Word of God is more important that the creation of God.

29. "Creation is secondary to the giving of the

Torah. [The rabbis say] if ever there were to be a moment that Torah was not studied on the earth, God would turn the universe back again into the primordial chaos, or void, that preceded the creation of the world."[18]

30. This emphasis of the importance of the Word of God carries over into the New Testament as the apostle Paul tells us to study with great passion the Word of Truth (2 Timothy 2:15), and that all Scripture comes from God (2 Timothy 3:16). John also emphasized the Word and said the Word became flesh in the person of Jesus (John 1)

31. The Midrash takes the word for "beginning" (*reishit*) as a synonym for "Torah" (Prov. 8:22), interpreting the first verse as declaring: "With *reishit* did God create the heaven and the earth." God created the world by consulting the Torah, fashioning a world based on Torah values, for the sake of the Torah, so that there would be somewhere in the universe where the values of the Torah could be put into practice (Genesis Rabbah 1:1, 6).[19]

32. Truth (אמת)

God has a plan for humanity. It involves understanding truth. The Hebrew word translated truth, is *emet* . Emet is comprised of the first, middle and last letters of the Hebrew alphabet. This means that truth (emet) encompasses the first, middle and last, or the totality of all that realized, or not realized. Jesus said, *"I am... truth" (John 14:6).*

33. Torah Fulfilled

God's ultimate plan is that His Messiah, His
Christ, will come and fulfill the Torah and
ultimately bring universal peace. According to
the ancients, even the name of Messiah spelled
backwards spells the name *Ha Shem*, meaning
"there will then live, the name of the Almighty."[20]

34. Even from the beginning of Genesis, the emphasis
points us to the Word, the Living Word, Jesus,
who will bring peace in the hearts of men and
ultimately bring universal peace.

35. The Lord said, "Think not that I am come to
destroy the law, or the prophets: I am not come to
destroy, but to fulfill" (Matthew 5:17 KJV). Also,
"In me (Jesus) ye might have peace. In the world
ye shall have tribulation: but be of good cheer; I
have overcome the world" (John 16:33 KJV).

The primordial light
(Messianic Light) created
then was so intense that
humans would have been able
to see everything happening
in the world. God realized
that humans could not endure
seeing reality that clearly. To
make the world tolerable for
human beings, God hid the
primordial light (Messianic
Light) until such time as
humans would be able to
stand it, replacing it with the
light of the sun.

CHAPTER TWO

THE SEVEN DAYS: GENESIS 1:2 – 2:3

A. The First Paragraph: The First Day 1:3-5

1. Verse 2 serves as an introduction to the six days of Creation. It shows the seven steps of God's creative work:

2. *And God said* – each day except the seventh begins with this phrase.

3. *Let there be* – is the authorization, approval, permission, or official sanction of *And God said.*

4. *And there was* – is the fulfillment of the authorization.

5. *And God made* – is the action itself described.

6. *And God called,* or *And God blessed* – is the act of naming or blessing.

7. *And God saw that it was good* – is God's evaluation, expressing diving satisfaction.

8. *And it was evening and it was morning of day* – is the finishing point, end or boundary.

9. Verse 2 also created a problem for some theologians that was remedied by the six-days of creation. *Tohu*, means "without form," emphasizing formlessness, was rectified in the first three days.

10. The verse describes a later catastrophe that overtook the original creation. The word "was" (*The earth was formless*) can be translated *"became"* – "The earth became, or had become formless and void."

    Support for this view of "later catastrophe" is seen in Isaiah 45:18 which describes the chaos, or catastrophe that overcame the earth. This was possibly one of the results of Lucifer's fall (Isaiah 14:12-17; Ezek. 28:11-19).

11. Paul seems to make an interesting use of the creation story. He says, "God who commanded the light to shine out of darkness hath shined in our hearts to give the light of the knowledge of the glory of God in the face of Jesus Christ" (2 Cor. 4:6 KJV).

12. We can seek in Genesis 1 a picture of fallen man, ruined by Satan, his intellect, emotions, and will all in a state of chaos, his conscience darkened, his body doomed to the dust.

    But he Spirit of God moves upon that darkness and begins a process of regeneration so that there emerges out of the chaos a new man, created in the image and likeness of the Son of God.[21]

13. Remember, Verse 2 created a problem, *Tohu*, means "without form," emphasizing formlessness, was rectified in the first three days. The first three days are days of division, or opposites.

> · First day: light and darkness
> · Second day; air/sky from water/sea
> · Third day: land and plants – all these remedy the problem of formlessness.

14. *Vohu,* meaning "empty" or "emptiness," was remedied in the second three days, or the days of decoration.

> · On the fourth day lights in the heavens provided ornamentation for the day and night that was created the first day
> · On the fifth day, fowl and fish are created to fill the air and sea created on the second day
> · On the sixth day, animals and man were created to occupy the dry land and plants created on the third day.

15. The above suggests in this first chapter of Genesis you find parallelism and symmetry. The work of the six days of creation came into being by the Word of God. God spoke, and it was so. All things came into being at God's Word. Psalm 33:3-9 affirms such.[22]

B. The Second Paragraph: The Second Day 1:6-8

1. In verse 5 you find *"one day"* – take by the
    Midrash to mean *"the day of the One."* The day
    on which God, whose name and essence are
    one, established a world suitable for the divine
    Presence (Gen. R. 3:1).[23]

2. Understanding there were no actual luminaries
    until the fourth "day" some conclude that the
    days referred to before the luminaries were "God-
    divided rather than sun-divided.[24] On this day,
    God was still the only spiritual being in existence,
    for the angels were not created until the second
    day (Rashi), according to Jewish tradition.[25]

3. The *"firmament"* or expanse is referring to the
    atmosphere that encircles our planet.

    "Sky" or heaven in Hebrew: *shamayim*. The
    Midrash (Gen. R. 4:7) understands the word as a
    combination of *esh* (fire) and *mayim* (water), that
    is, the sun and the rain clouds.

4. Were the rain clouds to extinguish the sun or were
    the sun to evaporate the rain clouds, the world
    would perish.

5. Therefore, God works a daily miracle. Fire
    and water agree to co-exist peacefully so that
    the world can endure. Another midrash (Deut.
    R. 1:12) links this idea to a passage in Jewish
    prayers:

"May you who establish peace in the heavens [teaching fire and water to get along] grant that kind of peace to us and to all the people Israel"

In other words, we pray for the miracle that both individuals and nations with the power to harm each other will learn to get along in peace – even as fire and water do in the heavens.[26]

6. On the second day we miss the formula "and God saw that it was good." The process of separating the waters were not concluded until the third day and one does not recite a blessing over an incomplete project (Rashi).

"God saw that it was good" occurs twice on the third day (vv. 10 and 12). As a result in Jewish tradition it is good luck to get married on Tuesday (the third day), or any other important occasions.

7. Genesis 1:7 describes the result of 1:6. God separated the atmospheric waters from the terrestrial waters by an arching expanse or the sky.

The result was the creation of the atmosphere. This verse may indicate that there was a canopy around the earth, but the text itself does not demand that a canopy be there.

8. The verse ends the phrase: *and it was so.* The Hebrew word here is *ken*. In modern Hebrew, it means "yes." In biblical Hebrew, it means "like an established thing."

It happened. It was so. It happened immediately after God's command. Elsewhere in the Old Testament, there are poetic descriptions of this particular act:

Job 37:18, He *spread out the sky [like] a molten mirror.*

Isaiah 40:22, He *stretches out the heavens as a curtain, and spreads them out as a tent to dwell in.*[27]

C. Third Paragraph: The Third Day 1:9-13

1. On the third day, two works were done. The first work is found in verses 9 – 10.

    Now there is a third separation: the separation of land and water (light and dark; waters and waters).

    So *dry land* appears for the first time, and there is a partial alleviation of the problem of 1:2 as *dry land* appears.

2. Verse 9 states: *gathered into one place* – it means there was land on one side and seas on the other. This shows that this event is dealing with something that came before the Continental Divide. It concludes: *and it was so.* (Here, God raised the continents from the deep).

3. In 1:10a is the naming, regarding the seas – The Hebrew reads: *mikveh hamayim*, meaning that

the waters were gathered into reservoirs (or pool – like a mikveh) *called...Seas* – this is the last thing God names in the creation account.

4.   Verse 10b gives the result: *and God saw that it was good.* This is the first of two times on the third day that He called something *good.* Only now is the work of the second day truly complete.

5.   In 1:11-12 we find the second work. The work itself is in verse 11. This is the creation of plant life. When it states: Let the earth put forth, or "sprout" it is not dealing with immediate creation – rather, at the command of God, the earth starts bringing forth its vegetation of some sort.

This is the provision of fertility for the earth, and God clothes the dry land with plants, trees, and grass.

6.   There are three divisions of the vegetable kingdom, all related to the Hebrew commandment: *Let the earth put forth, or sprout.*

The first term is *deshe eisev,* a general term that includes grass and grain – the word literally means "to vegetate vegetation."

The second category is *mazria zera,* literally meaning "seeding seed." This refers to herbs and vegetables.

The third category is *eitz pri,* which refers to fruit trees.

The species are now self-perpetuating – the result was: *and it was so.*

7.　In verse 12 *God saw that it was good* – For the second time on the third day: *God saw that it was good.*[28]

D. Fourth Paragraph: The Fourth Day 1:14-19

1.　Verse 14 marks the beginning of the fourth day. The purpose of the fourth day is to fill the work of the first day.

2.　This is the fourth division, the separation of the day from the night, and so these new lights will replace the light of 1:3.[29]

3.　The primordial light (Messianic Light) created then was so intense that humans would have been able to see everything happening in the world.

4.　For the same reason the seraphim covered their faces in Isaiah chapter six, as they could not look upon God's shekinah glory, or Messianic Light, God realized that humans could not endure seeing reality that clearly. To make the world tolerable for human beings, God hid the primordial light (Messianic Light) until such time as humans would be able to stand it (Rev. 21:1-6; 22:1-5), replacing it with the light of the sun (BT Hagigah 12a).[30]

5.   The purpose of the lights include:

First: *Let them be for signs* meaning navigational signs (Job 38:31-33 – constellations as signs; Psa. 19:1 – signs that declare the glory of God; Jer. 31:35, 36 – they are a sign of Israel's endlessness).

Second: *Let them be...for seasons.* The Hebrew word is *moadim*, which normally refers to regular religious festivals, but it also refers to temperature control. Religious festivals basically deal with the temperature time of spring and fall.

Third: Let them be *for days.* This refers to the earth's rotational axis, the twenty-four hour cycle and the interchange of day and night.

Fourth: Let them be for *years.* This refers to the earth's rotation around the sun. (Now that the sun has been created the earth can rotate on its axis for day and night and rotate in its orbit around the sun for the continuity of years).

Fifth: The main purpose was to provide light and to mark the passage of time in a very orderly fashion.[31] The result was *and it was so* (vs. 15).

6. Verses 16 – 18 then expands upon the results of verses 14 & 15.

    Greater & Lesser Lights (Sun & Moon, vs. 16): In Jewish tradition this insight of greater and lesser is used. Some stars are greater than the Sun, the Sun is greater than the moon – the moon reflects the light of the greater Sun.

7. The greatness of the Sun is a source of light, while the moon is small because it can only reflect what it receives from the sun.

8. In this sense, Jews pray at a *bris millah* (circumcision) "May this small one become great" – for a growing child is the recipient of wisdom and training from parents and teachers. They pray that the infant will grow up to become an independent source of greatness, who will enlighten others.[32]

9. *He made the stars also (16)* – With what astonishing brevity, too, God dismisses the creation of all the stars of space.

    He employs just five words – "He made the stars also." What a perspective of truth. The Bible takes some fifty chapters to discuss the construction and significance of the Tabernacle. Yet it was only a very temporary sanctuary.

10. Fifty chapters about the Tabernacle, five words about the stars. Truly the Bible looks at things from quite a different perspective from ours.

The Bible is a handbook of *redemption*, that is why. It was nothing for God to create; to create He had only to speak.

But to redeem, He had to suffer[33] (Rom. 11:33).

11. What a marvelous thought to ponder as you consider the billions of stars that exist. These five words reflect the sovereign creative ability of *God* (Hebrew, *"Elohim,"* making reference to His majestic power).

12. The phrase, *"He made the stars also,"* is like an after- thought, *"Oh, by the way, God* (Elohim) *created the stars also."*

From time to time, we need to be reminded that God is sovereign and has a plan for the universe and specifically your life.

13. The prophet Isaiah reminds us, *"Thus saith God the Lord, He that created the heavens, and stretched them out; He that spread forth the earth, and that which cometh out of it; He that giveth breath unto the people upon it, and spirit to them that walk therein: I, the Lord have called thee in righteousness, and will hold thine hand, and will keep thee..." (Isaiah 42:5,6 KJV).*

We can see in these verses that God has great concern and truly cares for His people. If God can create *"the stars also"* in all their glory and magnificence, can He not care for your concerns and needs?

14. David asks, *"What is man, that Thou art mindful of him? And the son of man, that Thou visitest him? For Thou hast made him a little lower than the angels, and hast crowned him with glory and honor"* (Psalm 8:4,5 KJV).

The term, *"mindful"* suggests that God is continually thinking about man. We are constantly on His mind. He has crowned those who trust in Him with glory and honor. One day believers in Jesus will be trophies of Grace eternally displayed before all creation (Ephesians 2:7).

15. David also states, with extreme pathos, *"I am poor and needy; yet the Lord thinketh upon me: Thou art my help and my deliverer; make no tarrying, O my God"* (Psalm 40:17 KJV).

The word "thinketh" (thinks) has the idea 'to regard and value.' Just as the parent or grandparent that carries photos of their children or grandchildren ready to show them at any moment. Constantly in the back of their mind, they are cherishing and regarding their "kids" or "grandkids." So it is with God and his children... He *thinks* upon us.

"For in Him we live and move and have our being." The Lord Jesus will never leave us nor forsake us. We are *"complete in Him'* who is *"all and in all"* (Acts 17:28; Hebrews 13:5; Colossians 2:10; 3:11).

Therefore, rest in the confidence that He who

"made the stars also" can complete that which He has started in you and will hold your hand; and keep you along the journey.[34]

The end result of the fourth day – *God saw that it was good.*

E. Fifth Paragraph: The Fifth Day 1:20-23

1. The purpose of the fifth day is to fulfill the work of the second day, which is the creation of sea and bird life.

    The Hebrew says *yishretzu sheretz* meaning "swarming with swarms."[35]

2. God created (Heb. *Bara*) – On the first day, it referred to Creation from a total vacuum; here, it refers to the huge size of some of the fish; and the last time it is used (vs. 27) it refers to the Creation of Man, intelligent life in the image of God.[36]

3. Sea monsters: the Hebrew word is *tannin* and the word "Leviathan." These words appear in Canaanite myths regarding a dragon god from earliest times who assisted Yam (god of the sea) in a battle against Baal (Canaanite god of fertility).

    By stating that they were part of God's creation (*bara*), the narrative deprives them of divinity.

4. Then God blessed them to multiply. There was

a legend that Tannin lived in the deepest part of the sea and supported the earth on its back and every seventy years, it lifted up its tail, causing earthquakes. It was not allowed to have a mate because if it had offspring they would overpower the world.

5. To defuse this fanciful tale Moses penned, *"God blessed them, saying, be fruitful and multiply and fill the waters in the seas."* (Praise the Lord from the earth, Sea monsters and all deeps, Psa. 148:7).

    The rabbis declare that the sea creatures and birds needed a special blessing because many of them would be caught and destroyed.[37]

6. Man's domain is being prepared for him. The seas were filled with fish and the skies were filled with fowl – an interesting combination.

7. Fish and fowl have much in common. Both have streamlined forms to enable them to move swiftly through their native habitats, both are covered with shingle-like layers of protective fins or feathers, both have hollow, light bones, both lay eggs, and both have migratory instincts.

8. Water is preeminently the seat of life. There is not a by or creek, not a shelf or a sound on the face of the earth that does not teem with life.

    Even a drop of ditch water can hold 500 million microscopic creatures so small that a teaspoonful full of water would be to them what the Atlantic is to us.

9. Only a God who is infinite could have worked on such a majestic scale as we see in the skies and on such a microscopic scale as we see in the seas. There is no such thing as bigness or smallness to a God who is infinite.[38]

F. Sixth Paragraph: The Sixth Day 1:24-31

1. God made His final preparation of the earth as man's domain. He made three categories of land animals:

   First: *Cattle*, is a general term for all domesticated animals including cows, bulls, sheep, goats, rams, etc.

   Second: *Creeping things*, which include both large and small animals without legs, or with very short legs so that they appear to walk on their bellies, such as reptiles and amphibians.

   Third: *Beasts of the earth*, wild animals that cannot be domesticated.

   The conclusion was *and God saw that it was good.*[39]

2. Scientists have classified millions of different species of animals, including more than 800,000 different kinds of insects, 30,000 kinds of fish, 9,000 kinds of birds, 6,000 kinds of reptiles, 3,000 kinds of amphibians, and 5,000 kinds of mammals.

3.   Where did all this bewildering variety of life form
     come from? The same God who with fantastic
     abundance and full generosity tossed out into
     intangible space countless stars and their satellites
     – and who keeps them whirling and plunging on
     their journeys through space at inconceivable
     velocities, yet with such mathematic precision
     that we can tell the occasion of an eclipse or the
     visit of a comet years in advance – the same God
     who did that, with equal boundless generosity
     selected a single planet and filled it with a
     bewildering number of forms of life.

4.   If Genesis 1 were a psalm, it would have doubtless
     concluded with a resounding "Selah" – There.
     What do you think of that![40]

5.   So far the account of Creation has altered
     between events regarding the heavens and events
     regarding the earth. Now the Torah turns to the
     events regarding the creation of human beings –
     a combination of the heavens and the earthy, the
     sublime and the physical.[41]

6.   The three words, *Let us make*, make up one
     Hebrew word, *naaseh*, which is the jussive
     form, or mood, expressing a command – which
     is different from *Let there be (yehi)* which is
     a cohortative form, or mood, that expresses
     encouragement or exhortation. The change tells
     us something profound is about to happen.

7.   The use of the plural pronoun *Let us*, opens the
     door to the plurality in the Godhead, as was true
     with the word *Elohim*.

8. The rabbis teach that God was speaking to angels – however the text never indicates angels were part of the conversation.

9. If God had consulted, it would have said so as in the case of 1 kings 22:19-23, where God consulted with the heavenly court about doing something.[42]

10. In our image, in Hebrew is one word *betzalmeinu*. The root is *tzalam*, and refers to the original image or imitation. This same word is also used of idols.[43]

11. In the ancient Near East, the ruling king was often described as the "image" or the "likeness" of a god which served to elevate the monarch above ordinary mortals.

12. In the Bible, this idea became democratized. Every human being is created "in the image of God"; each bears the stamp of royalty. Thus the description of mortals as 'in the image of God" makes humankind the symbol of God's presence on earth.[44]

13. This preamble (*Let us make man*) indicates that Man was created with great deliberation – that Man was brought into being with the deepest involvement of Divine Providence and wisdom.[45]

14. In our image, or in Our mold (Rashi) meaning that God had prepared the mold with which He would now shape Man – Throughout the chapter, God

brought all things into being with an utterance, but He created Man with His own hands as it were (Rashi).[46]

15. *According (after) our likeness* is one Hebrew word *kidmuteinu* which means "a model" or "a copy." This also emphasizes the uniqueness of human beings (Psa. 8:3-5).

16. Man is in no way related to the beasts.

What animal can transmit accumulated achievements from one generation to another?

What animal experiences a true sense of guilt when it does wrong or has a developed consciousness of judgment to come?

What animal shows any desire to worship?

What animal has hope of immortality beyond the grave?

What beast can exercise abstract moral judgment or show appreciation of the beauties of nature?

When did we ever see a dog admiring a sunset or a horse standing breathless before the rugged grandeur of a mountain range?

What animal ever learned to read and write, to act with deliberate purpose, and set goals and achieve long range objectives?

What animal ever learned to cook its food, to cut cloth and make clothes, or invent elaborate tools?

What animal ever enjoyed a hearty laugh?

What animal has the gift for speech?

Even the most primitive human tribe possesses linguistics of a subtle, complex and eloquent nature. Man stands alone.

17. *Physically*, he alone of all the creatures on the globe, walks upright; *mentally*, he alone has the ability to communicate in a sophisticated manner; *spiritually*, he alone has the capacity to know the mind and will of God.[47]

18. Man, *Adam* the name given to the first human being, is now a general term used for all human beings, is to *rule or have dominion* over all that has been created by God.

19. God created man – He created him – He created them (27). The word *bara* is used three times to emphasize that a high point was reached here – a profound moment. (Remember *bara* is a word only used of God and of the work that only God can do – never used with anything man does).

- Man's creation
- Created in the divine image
- Both man and woman were created on the sixth day and both were created in the image of God

20. Genesis 1:28-30 presents the Edenic Covenant, which is the first of eight covenants of the Bible.

(Edenic Covenant, Gen. 1:28-30; 2:15-17; *Adamic Covenant,* Gen. 3:14-19; *Noahic Covenant,* Gen. 8:20-9:170; *Abrahamic Covenant,* Gen. 12:1-3; *Mosaic Covenant,* Exod. 20-23; Deuteronomy; *Davidic Covenant,* 2 Sam. 7:4-17; *Land Covenant,* Deut. 30:1-10; *New Covenant,* Jer. 31:31-37.

21. The Edenic Covenant spelled out in two parts:

The first part, (1:28-30), begins with the blessing of verse 28a: *And God blessed them.*

This covenant is made between God and Adam, and Adam stands as the representative head of the human race (Hosea 6:7 refers to this).

The second part, (vv. 28b – 30) list four specific provisions of the Edenic covenant.

Provision one: Populate the earth. The earth is to be filled with humanity. This shows that sexual intercourse was not the first sin; it is actually commanded here, because it is by sexual intercourse that humanity reproduces itself.

Provision two: Subdue (have authority) over the material world. Previously, this authority was given to Satan (Ezek. 28:11-19), but Satan lost it when he fell. So now Satan is replaced, and the authority of the physical earth is given to man.

Provision three: Rule over (have dominion over) all living things – over the animal kingdom (creatures in the sea, air, and upon the dry ground).

Provision four: Human diet – vegetables, or vegetarianism. At this point, man was to be strictly vegetarian for obvious reasons; to eat animal food requires the death of the animal, and physical death can only come following Adam's fall. This diet was also true for the animal kingdom as well (30) – *and it was so.*

22. In verse 31 God saw all that He had made during the six days – everything He made. The verdict was: *and, behold, it was very good,* not merely *good,* but now the word *very* is added.

23. *The sixth day:* For the first time, there is the use of the definite article, not *a sixth day,* as was the case with all the others, but it is *the* sixth day.

24. This is the second time that uniqueness is emphasized the sixth day – the third indication of its uniqueness is that it happens to be the most detailed of the days given.[48]

G. Seventh Paragraph: The Seventh Day 2:1-3

1. Verse one summarizes the completion of all work of the six days. The summary emphasizes five things: Finishing, completion, cessation, blessing, and sanctifying.

2. Geneses 2:2 declares the cessation of the creation. God finished his creative work. From now on, it is no longer creation, but procreation. God abstained from work on the seventh day.[49]

3. The creation was complete. There is a great satisfaction in surveying a finished work. God stood back, as it were, to cast an admiring, contented eye over the finished work of His hands – the Creator was content.[50]

4. The Hebrew word for rested is *shabbat*, which means "to complete," "to cease," "to rest." So God *rested*, not in the sense of recuperating from tiredness, but God *rested* in the sense of cessation at having completed or finished His work.

5. The word *shabbat* here is not used as a proper name for the seventh day, because the word *shabbat* here is a verb, not a noun. It is not used as a noun or a proper name for the seventh day until the Exodus, because only then is the command to keep the Sabbath actually given.[51]

6. Ten times in verses 2 and 3 God is mentioned as though to emphasize the fact that it was God's Sabbath. Later on He extended it to Israel as part of His covenant with the Jewish people (Exodus 20).[52] The Edenic Covenant contained no commandment to Adam and Eve to keep the seventh day as a day of rest. The point of this verse is that God ceased from His creative activity.[53]

7. The word *sanctified* or *hallowed* means "to set apart, and so there is elevation and exultation. However, this first use of the biblical concept of holiness relates to time.[54]

    Therefore, God ceased His creative work on that day from that which He *created (bara)* and from that which He had *made (asah)*.

8. Later in Israel's history, God's resting on the seventh day becomes the basis of keeping the Sabbath (Exod. 31:17): *on the seventh day God rested (ceased), and was refreshed.*

9. Some observations of this section (Gen.2:1-3) are in order, one of which is the usage of the numbers three and seven.

    First: The Hebrew text has thirty-five words, which is a multiple of five times seven.

    Second: Verses 2 through 3a contain three sentences, and each of these three sentences contains seven words.

    Third: The exact middle expression is the seventh day, emphasizing the figure seven.

    Fourth: The three middle clauses (2a, 2b, 3a) have seven words each, and the word seventh is within each of the phrases.

    Fifth: The phrase his work is found three times. A rabbinic teach about this passage states:

> The Sabbath parallels the world to come, a
> time of complete good and tranquility for
> those who are worthy of it.[55]

10. Below Fruchtenbaum brilliantly charts a few New
Testament quotations and applications of Genesis
1:1 – 2:2 that can be made:

Applications from the Creation Account[56]

Genesis	New Testament	Applications
Messiah as Creator and Redeemer		
1:1-5	John 1:1-5	Messiah as Creator and the Light of men
Ch. 1	Col. 1:15-20	-Messiah as the image of God
		-Messiah as the Creator
		-Messiah as before all things
		-Messiah as the beginning of the new Body, the Church
		-Messiah having all the fullness of God
		-Messiah as reconciler of all things on earth and in heaven
The Messiah as the Image of God		
1:26	2 Cor. 4:4	Messiah as the image of God; "the glory of Christ, Who is the image of God"
	Phil. 2:6	Christ being "in the form of God"
	Col. 1:15	Christ as "the image" of the "invisible God"
	Heb. 1:3	Christ as "the very image" of God
Man in the Image of God		
1:26	1 Cor. 11:7	Man is the image and glory of God
	Jas. 3:6	Man was made in "the likeness of God"
Believers as in the Image of Christ		
1:26	Rom. 8:29	Believers are being "conformed to the image of his Son"
	1 Cor. 15:49	Believers shall bear "the image" of the man in heaven
	2 Cor. 3:18	Believers are being changed into Christ's likeness

	Col. 3:10	The new nature is "being renewed... after the Image" of its Creator
	God's Original Purpose:	
1:27	Matt. 9:4	The permanency of marriage
	Mark 10:6	The permanency of marriage
	Gal. 3:28	The way of salvation is the same for both male And female
	Rest	
2:2	Hebrews 4:4	The seventh day rest as the rest of faith and heavenly rest

11. The rabbis say the Sabbath is sanctified above the normal course of physical activity in this world. Ordinarily, people must work to earn their livelihood, but on the Sabbath, work is forbidden – and even so the Sabbath is a day that is blessed with more food and enjoyment than the rest of the week, referring to the double portion of manna given on Friday (Exodus 16:4).[57]

12. Today we rest, not on a special day but in a Person. Our double portion is found in Christ – we rest where God rests – in Messiah Yeshua and His finished work.

So there remains a Sabbath rest for the people of God. For the one who has entered His rest has himself also rested from his works, as God did from His. Therefore, let us be diligent to enter that rest (Hebrews 4:9-11a).

Come to Me all who are weary and heavy-laden, and I will give you rest (Matt. 11:28).

Man's "glory and freedom"
is dependent upon God.
Human sovereignty can
never quite be absolute. It
must always be subject to the
demands of a higher law, the
divinely ordained moral order
of the universe.

CHAPTER THREE

HISTORY (*TOLDOT*) OF THE HEAVENS AND EARTH: GENESIS 2:4 - 2:7

A. Introduction to the history 2:4

1. The Lord God – This is the unspoken, unique, holy, personal divine name YHVH (יהוה) of God. Elohim (אלהים), the general term of God, is used many times, YHVH is used here in verse four and again in the Torah found in Exodus 9:30.

2. The first *toldot* is sometimes called "The Tablet of Adam." As earlier stated, the *toldot* tells us "what became of," in this case what became of *the heavens and of the earth* that God had *created.* What became of them is that they were cursed through disobedience, and so decay began spreading rapidly in the human race. Whereas in the creation account, God blessed three times; now in this *toldot*, He will curse three times.[58]

3. Genesis 2:4 states: *in the day.* Here the Hebrew word is *yom* is used without a numeral, and

without a numeral it can refer to a longer period of time. It is used for a period of time here because this *yom* includes all seven days. However [the idea is], with a numeral it means twenty-four hours.[59]

4. The theology of this section teaches several things.

    First, man has the capacity to serve God.

    Second, man is responsible to obey God's Word, which was used to create the universe.

    Third, God gave man the institution of marriage.

    Fourth, this section emphasizes man over creation in general, and so it gives us details on the creation of man and details on man's nature as God's image.

    Fifth, God's special care and provision for man and woman is related in that He gives them a garden to live in, gives them special work to do such as naming the animals, and He provides Eve for Adam.

    Sixth, God does not forsake His creation.[60]

5. The Name יהוה also signifies the eternity of God, because its letters are also those of the words:

    היה – He was
    הוה – is
    ויהיה – will be

6. The Four-letter Name is often translated the Eternal One. This is also the proper Name of God. In respect for its intense holiness, it is not pronounced as it is spelled. In prayer or when reciting a complete Scriptural verse, it is pronounced Adonai. Otherwise, it is referred to as HASHEM, or the Name.[61]

7. *These are the "toldot" (generations, history, account) of the heavens and the earth when they were created.*

   The *Midrash Rabbah* contains an unusual Messianic interpretation that is worth retelling simply for the sake of its novelty.

   In *Genesis Rabbah* 12:6, the Sages point out that the word "generations" (toldot, תולדות) in Genesis 2:4 is spelled with two *vavim* (ו). In all other instances, except for one in the book of Ruth, the word is spelled with only one *vav* (תולדת).

8. Since the sages assumed that every letter of Torah is significant (even Yeshua taught that every jot and tittle is eternal), they searched tiny discrepancies like this for meaning.

   In this case, they explain that prior to Adam's sin, the word "generations" (toldot) was spelled with two *vavim* (תולדות) to indicate that the generations of Adam and the generations of all creation were complete and whole.

9. But subsequent to sin, those generations were diminished. Their diminution is indicated by the defective spelling of the word of toldot (תולדת). Adam's sin affected even the heavens and the earth.

> *Rabbi Berekiah said in the name of Rabbi Shmuel bar Nachman, "Though these things were created in their fullness, yet when Adam sinned they were spoiled, and they will not be restored to their fullness until the Son of Perez [i.e. the Messiah] comes, as it says [in Ruth 4:18], "Now these are the generations (toldot, תולדות) of Perez."* (Genesis Rabbah 12:6)

10. Rabbi Berekiah sees a Messianic meaning in this restored spelling. Messiah is the one who will restore both the generations of mankind and the generations of the whole creation. He calls Messiah the "Son of Perez" because in Ruth 4:18, *Perez* stands at the head of David's genealogy – the *toldot* of the Davidic monarchy from which Messiah comes.

But can we really speak of the creation having "generations"? Do the heavens and the earth beget children? Yes, Paul speaks of the creation groaning in childbirth, awaiting the redemption along with us (Romans 8:20-22).[62]

B. Creation of Man 2:5-7

1. **Vs. 5:** *[HASHEM]* God had not sent rain because there was no man to work the soil. But when

Adam was created, he recognized its importance for the world.

He prayed, and rain fell, causing the trees and vegetation to spring forth (Rashi).

As noted [previously] plant life had already been created and was waiting just below the surface for Adam to pray – The Talmudic sage Rav Assi noted the apparent contradiction between 1:12 (earth brought forth vegetation) & 2:5 (that nothing had grown prior to the creation of Adam) [was] that the herbs began to grow on the third day, as they had been commanded, but stopped before they broke through the soil. It remained for Adam to pray for them, whereupon rain fell, and the growth was completed. This teaches that God longs for the prayers of the righteous (Chullin 60b).

2. This demonstrates a basic article of faith (within Judaism): God provides what Man needs, but it is up to Man to pray and otherwise carry out his spiritual responsibilities.

    As the Sages say regarding the Matriarchs: Sarah, Rebecca, Rachel and Leah were each, by nature, incapable of bearing children. God created them that way because He knew that they and their husbands would pray for children, and God desires the prayers of the righteous.[63]

3. *No shrub in the field* describes the initial state of the earth after dry land appeared as recorded in Gen. 1:9-10.

Rain is not only a natural phenomenon it is also a "blessing" from God.

4. *No man to cultivate the ground* – Agriculture is regarded as the original vocation of human beings; the earth is integral to their being.[64]

5. **Vs. 6:** God caused the deep (subterranean waters) to rise, (moistening the dry earth), forming low-flying clouds filled with water to moisten the dust (arid earth), from which Adam was created. It is similar to a kneader who first pours in water and then kneads the dough. Here too: *First, He watered the soil, and then He formed Man (Rashi)*[65]

6. **Vs. 7:** *Dust* is a word that can be used synonymously with "clay." The verb "formed" (va-yitzer) is often used in the Bible to describe the activity of a potter (yotzer).[66]

7. *Yitzer* (formed) is used here, whereas, in Chapter one, *Bara* (created) was used. *Bara* emphasizes something only God can do – that is create something out of nothing. *Yitzer* (formed) emphasizes "to mold" or "shape by design" out of something – *"dust."* Although, man was created out of something, it was only something that God could do.

    Yitzer is used of a potter shaping clay (Isa. 29:16, Jer. 18:1-17); goldsmiths who make idols (Isa. 44:9, Hab. 2:18); regarding the shaping of Messiah's body in the womb (Isa. 49:5); also, where God forms hearts (Psa. 33:15); the eye (Psa. 94:9); and when God formed man (Psa. 119:73).

8. Genesis 2:7 the word *yitzer* is written with two *yods* (יי), וייצר. In 2:19, it is written properly with one *yod* (י), ויצר. Rabbis suggest a few explanations for the inconsistency regarding spelling: first, the two yods represent the two inclinations: the good inclination and the evil inclination; second, or it refers to the creation of both the material and the immaterial; third, or it refers to a double forming, one for this world, and one for the resurrection.[67] This symbol is evocative of the notion of God's absolute mastery over man (Isa. 29:16; 45:9).[68]

9. Man's "glory and freedom" is dependent upon God. Human sovereignty can never quite be absolute. It must always be subject to the demands of a higher law, the divinely ordained moral order of the universe.[69]

10. J.I. Packer states, "What were we made for? To know God. What aim should we set ourselves in life? To know God. What is the 'eternal life' that Jesus gives? Knowledge of God. *'This is life eternal, that they might know thee the only true God, and Jesus Christ, whom thou hast sent' (John 17:3).* What is the best thing in life, bringing more joy, delight and contentment than anything else? Knowledge of God (Jeremiah 9:23,24). What, of all the states God ever sees man in, gives God most pleasure? Knowledge of Himself. *'For I desired mercy, and not sacrifice;*

and the knowledge of God more than burnt offerings'" (Hosea 6:6 NKJV).[70]

11. One scholar makes this observation of the Hebrew word "life" (Chaim or Hayyim or HYYM, no vowels in Hebrew, simply vowel sounds). The word for life in Hebrew ends with (YiM), the indicator of plurality. We are granted not one life, but two.

12. For life, to be true life, it cannot be lived alone. This speaks of the need for community. Not only do we need the support of each other in the Body of Christ, this speaks of a greater need. The plurality of the Hebrew word for life suggests we are granted not one life, but two. We are granted two lives – one here on earth, and the other in eternity. In terms of eternity, the Scriptures speak of two eternal places of existence, namely heaven and hell.

13. Both in Hebrew as well as in English, the words (HaYYiM) and life each contain four letters. Central to the English word for existence, surrounded by the first and last letter, is the word *'if'*. Life is subject to imponderables. We are the prey of forces beyond our control. Central to the word (HaYYiM, חיים), the Hebrew word for life, are two *yods* (YY, יי), which combined form the name of *God*.

14. Rabbis are known for their conjectures and interpretation of every letter in Hebrew Scripture; however, to do this in the English rendering

doesn't work very well. Nevertheless for our purpose in explaining the significance of God, belief in the Almighty replaces the great *'if'* of life. When *God* is central to our lives, doubt and despair are replaced by confidence and divine comfort – *God* is the greater need. Central to the Hebrew word for life is the name of God.[71]

15. *Man...Ground* – In Hebrew is *Adam* (אדם) & *Adamah* (ארמה) a word play emphasizing man's earthly origin.

16. *The Breath of Life* – Genesis 2:7b deals with the immaterial part of man. In Hebrew it is *nishmat chaim* (נשמת חיים). This is the *neshamah*, or the breath of God; and the word is used twenty-five times in the Old Testament.

17. God's breath brings animation, causing man to become a *living soul*. In Job 32:8, it also brings spiritual understanding. Therefore, the result is moral capacity.[72]

18. The Hebrew word *ruach* (spirit, wind) is used of God, man, animal, and idols, the word *neshamah* is used only of God and man, except once, where it is used of animals in Genesis 7:22.

19. It is this breath of God, the *neshamah*, that produced the life of man. According to Job 34:14-15, if God took back His Spirit and His breath, all flesh would perish together, and man would return to dust (Psa. 104:29; Isa. 2:22).

20. The *neshamah* is also found in animals (Gen.
    7:22), but only to man is it directly given. Only
    in man does it say that *God breathed into his
    nostrils the breath of life*, making man somewhat
    distinct from the animal kingdom in that man is
    eternal, and animals are not eternal.

21. This means that not only is man physical, man is
    also spirit. The result of this "breathing in" was;
    and man became a living soul. The living soul
    in Hebrew is *nephesh chayah*. This concept of
    living soul is also found in animals (Gen. 1:24,
    30; 2:19) but, like the spirit, the soul of man is far
    more complex and eternal than the animal.

22. First Corinthians 15:45 mentions that the first
    man, Adam, was made a living soul, and this is
    based upon this particular passage. Therefore,
    man's uniqueness does not lie in the fact of the
    breath of life as such, because the same words
    are used of the animal kingdom. However, man's
    uniqueness lies in the fact that he has the image of
    God, and the animal kingdom does not.[73] "Thus
    the human being is a combination of the earthly
    and the divine" (Rashi).[74]

23. And He blew into his nostrils the soul of life.
    God thus made Man out of both lower (earthly)
    and upper (heavenly) matter: his body from the
    dust and his soul from the spirit (Rashi).[75]

    The Jewish sages state, *"one who blows, blows
    from within himself,"* indicating that Man's soul
    is part of God's essence, as it were.[76]

24. *Soul* derives from the Hebrew root *"Nephesh"* which has several connotations:

   a. *Breath, or the Principle of Life*: When this breath is absent there is death. At death the spirit is departed.

   b. *Mind and Rationality*: The idea is that the soul not only discovers the trustworthy but persuades the whole person to place his trust in it or cast his all upon it.

   c. *The seat of Affections, Feelings and Emotions*:

       The soul, which the Lord breathed into the body, feels after the Lord and upon discovering Him is moved to rejoice in Him.

   d. *It Signifies a Person*: That which can love or hate; that which can sing or be sad; that which can be excited by the right or by the wrong makes up the total personality.[77]

25. The soul, the breath of God, came from God and through faith in Jesus Christ it returns to spend eternity with its divine source.[78]

   You are different from the beasts of the field by virtue of your "intellect, free will, self-awareness, consciousness of the existence of others, conscience, responsibility and self-control.[79]

   Being created 'in the image of God' implies that human life is infinitely precious.[80]

   David exclaimed, *"I am fearfully and wonderfully made" (Psalm 139:14).*

Moses wrote the Book of
Genesis. He was not an
eyewitness to the events
written within the book – he
was a researcher compiling
oral and written traditions
and in the end editor of the
information. However, he was
an eyewitness when writing
Exodus, Leviticus, Numbers
and Deuteronomy (with
exception of his birth, death
and subsequent events).

APPENDIX

A. Regarding Hebrew

The Hebrew Alphabet is called *aleph-bet* and is read from right to left (English is read from left to right). The aleph-bet consists of 22 letters – all consonants. There are no vowels in the Hebrew alphabet, only vowel sounds of dots and dashes (nikkudim) placed above or below the consonants. These "nikkudim" were added by the Masoretes (7th – 10th centuries A.D.) for continuity in chanting scripture in the synagogues.

Originally, Hebrew was formed to depict word pictures. The *aleph*, the first letter of the aleph-bet, was the head of an ox.

$$\aleph \quad \left|\begin{matrix}\text{Alef}\\\text{(silent)}\end{matrix}\right| \quad \eth \; 0 \; \flat \; \times$$

Tav, the last letter was an X or plus sign, a cross.

$$\daleth \quad \left|\begin{matrix}\text{Tav}\\\text{(T)}\end{matrix}\right| \quad \phi \; \phi + \; \chi$$

The Zohar (Jewish mystical teaching) believes that the *tav* makes an impression regarding the Ancient of Days – that the impression of the *tav* is the secret of the power that links worlds – generations – together. The initial impression of true faith was that which was stamped upon the soul of our first father, Abraham, "the first of all believers" (Jewish Mysticism and

79

Thought, based on the teachings of Harav Yitzchak Ginsburgh – *note: the Zohar is full of fanciful teachings that cannot be esteemed as complete truth or equal to scripture. Simply, it is Jewish mysticism. Some of the components are interesting such as mentioned above).*

Some believe that the aleph-bet secretly, mysteriously, told of God's redemption plan? The plan began with animal sacrifices and ended at the cross. Some rabbis would disagree.

Sidenote: Bereishit bara Elohim et hashamayim ve'et ha'arets – *In the beginning God created the heaven and the earth.* The middle word of the seven Hebrew words is *"et"* – the aleph and the tav. –the Messiah??

Light (Gen. 1:3) represents the Shekinah, or light of Messiah.

משיח   Messiah – MeSSiaH – MSH – Jesus

השם   HaShem – HaSHeM – HS(H)M – God

        Messiah is God – God is Messiah
        Jesus is Messiah – Jesus is God

אמת   Truth – EMeT – first, middle, last letters of Hebrew alphabet.

From birth to death. That is the ultimate truth of every human being. The three letters EMeT may be read in two combinations of beginning and end:

      אמת: Truth
      אם EM – Mother
      מת MeT – Death

From the cradle to the grave – these are the unavoidable boundaries of our human existence. To know this truth is the first step for making the most of ourselves during the time we are granted by the Almighty on this earth.

That which is true is everlasting. Truth requires for its essence the first letter א (alef), the "One" standing for the Almighty. Remove this intial letter in אמת (EMeT) and all that remains is מת (MeT).

Without God there can be no truth. In its place only death and destruction remain [Blech: 1991:62,64,65].

The first letter א (alef), representing the Almighty, or the Messiah, was the "Ox," or the sacrifice for the sins of mankind.

Jesus said, "I am the way, and the truth, and the life" (John 14:6).

B. Two Questions

1. Question: *Moses wrote Genesis by research – is there anything in Egyptology that could be construed to be reflected in the text as opposed to the revelation of God?*

Answer: Along with what was mentioned earlier regarding the fifth day concerning sea monsters and the Canaanite myths of a dragon god Moses also addressed Egypt's creator god Khnum. By emphasizing God as a potter and creator, one who gives life, soul and flesh from the "dust," he deprives Khnum of divinity.

Khnum (Khnemu, Khenmu, Khenmew, Chnum) was one of the most ancient gods of Egypt, whose worship is thought to have been popular as early as the Predynastic Period (5,500-3,100 BC). References from the Pyramid Texts of Unas confirm that his worship was long established even at that early stage and the Old Kingdom pharaoh Khufu (the builder of the Great Pyramid) was actually called "Khnum-Khufu" ("Khnum is his Protector").

As well as creating the body and the "ka" (spirit), before the birth of each newborn child, he could bless the child with good health.

His role changed from river god to the one who made sure that the right amount of silt was released into the water during the inundation. In working with the silt, the very soil that the ancient Egyptian potters used, he became the great potter who not only molded men and women, but who molded the gods themselves and the world, and was thought to have created the pharaoh's form and soul on his potter's wheel.

Pottery was created out of the soil of the Nile, and it was believed that he created the first humans - and the gods - on his potter's wheel with this silt, and thus was a creator god who was 'Father of the Fathers of the Gods and Goddesses, Lord of Created Things from Himself, Maker of Heaven and Earth and the Duat (book of the dead) and Water and the Mountains'.

2. Question: (Though not directly addressed in the lecture series the following question was asked by a student. Genesis chapter six will be addressed more fully in a subsequent lecture) *In Genesis 6:6 the Bible says that God repented that He had made man. I've heard preachers say that God changed His mind. Since He is the same: yesterday, today and forever, how can it be that He "changed" His mind?*

Answer: Genesis 6:5-7 records the judgment of God.

Verse 5 explains why the judgment was proclaimed: the wickedness of man. Man was unable to control sin.

Then the Lord saw – God here is evaluating humanity. In His evaluation He saw two things: first, man's external sin was great throughout the earth; second, man's internal sin, thoughts and imagination was also great throughout the earth.

Every intent (imagination) – the word "every" emphasizes the fact that sin was prevalent, widespread in all areas of society.

Intent (imagination) – intent, or imagination, is the Hebrew *yatzar* (yitzer) – same word used in 2:7, referencing God's forming of man. The idea is: God formed man by holy design, but man took its God-given abilities to devise or design evil continually.

Verse 6 records God's response and pain.

a. Response: God repented that He had made man because man had negated God's purpose in creation. Repented, regretted, or reconsidered refers to a change in God's actions, resulting from a change in man's actions.

For example, in 1 Samuel 15:11, God regretted that He made Saul king & in 1 Samuel 15:29 the record states, that God does not change His mind – is there a contradiction?

Only from man's perspective does God seem to change His mind. God seems to change His mind because man has changed his attitude toward Him (1 Sam. 15:11).

God responds to man in one way when man obeys and He responds another way when man disobeys – Saul was obedient; and God made him king. Then Saul became disobedient, so God removed the kingship from him.

It appears from man's perspective that God changed His mind – basically, no change took place. God responds one way to obedience, and He responds another way to disobedience.

The Hebrew word for repent here is *nacham* – the same root as *Noah*, and the actual meaning is "to comfort" (Gen. 5:29), So literally it reads "God was comforted," meaning God was comforted in the sense of being justified in executing judgment, because the sin of man requires judgment from God.

b.   Pain: It grieved God's heart, it saddened Him because of man's action and God's reaction, to man's action, that was about to be made.

Three Hebrew terms are found in 5:29 & 6:6:
Nacham – translated "comfort" (5:29) & "repent" (6:6).

Etzev – translated "toil" (5:29) & "grieve" (6:6).

Asah – translated "work" (5:29) & "made" (6:6).

So there is a bridge between what happens in 5:29 in reference to Noah and what sets the stage for the Flood judgment.

Verse 7 God gives an ominous statement that He will destroy all living creatures that breath air.

Verse 8 gives hope in the face of judgment: *Noah found (grace) favor in the eyes of the Lord.*

The word *found* shows favor (grace) is not won, and it is not earned. It is simply found in God – the reason given is discovered in verse 9 and in 7:1.

God's actions, once again, responded to a man's action. God did not change His mind regarding 'Blotting out man from the face of the earth.–simply, Noah was a righteous man – God responded accordingly.

For life, to be true life,
it cannot be lived alone.
This speaks of the need for
community. Not only do
we need the support of each
other in the Body of Christ,
this speaks of a greater need.
The plurality of the Hebrew
word for life suggests we are
granted not one life, but two.
We are granted two lives – one
here on earth, and the other in
eternity. In terms of eternity,
the Scriptures speak of two
eternal places of existence,
namely heaven and hell.

LECTURES IN GENESIS
STUDENT'S NOTES

GENESIS 1:1 – 2:7

Jeffrey D. Johnson, PhD

Lectures in Genesis Student's Notes: (Teacher may photo copy notes for students)

Genesis 1:1 – 2:7

Jeffrey D. Johnson, PhD

www.israeltodayministries.org

Genesis Introduction

*May he kiss me with the kisses of
his mouth (Song of Songs 1:2)*

A Kiss From God

1. Kissing only occurs in close, face-to-face relationships.

2. The Scripture tells us that God spoke to Moses *p'anim al p'anim*, face to face suggesting intimacy (Exod. 33:11; Hebrews 1:1, 2).

3. What is a kiss from God? (Song of Songs Rabbah 2:2,1; Targum to the Song of Songs, Ch. 1, v. 2).

4. An "aha!" moment!

*May God kiss you with a thousand kisses during
our study of Genesis!*

A. Title

1. Bereishit (Hebrew, בראשית)

    "In the beginning." Originally, call *Sepher Maaseh Bereishit*, meaning "The Book of the Act of In the Beginning."

2. Geneseos (Greek)

    In the Greek translation of the Old Testament (Septuagint) the first book of the Bible is called *Geneseos,* which is the Greek translation for the

Hebrew word *toldot*, which is the English word *generations*. The Greek name means "The Book of Origins."

3. Genesis (English)

    Genesis comes from the Greek *geneseos* and also means "The Book of Origins."

B. Author

1. Moses wrote the Book of Genesis.

2. Genesis is a compilation of eleven histories (Heb. Toldot). *Toldot* means generations, genealogy, or history of people or events – simply a family document.

3. Eleven Histories (Toldot, what became of, what happened?):

    1) Heavens and earth (2:4 – 4:26).
    2) Adam (5:1 – 6:8).
    3) Noah (6:9 – 9:29).
    4) Sons of Noah (10:1 – 11:9)
    5) Shem (11:10-26).
    6) Terah (11:27 – 25:11).
    7) Ishmael (25:12-18).
    8) Isaac (25:19 – 35:29).
    9) Esau, what became of Esau (36:1-8).
    10) Esau, what became of Esau as the father of the Edomites (36:9 – 37:1).
    11) Jacob (37:2 – 50:26).

4. In the story of Creation the number seven occurs again and again.

5. Seven paragraphs – seven days.

6. *And there was evening and there was morning, such-and-such a day.* The Masoretes were right.

7. * First Paragraph: (1:2-5).
    * Second Paragraph: (1:6-8).
    * Third Paragraph: (1:9-13).
    * Fourth Paragraph: (1:14-19).
    * Fifth Paragraph: (1:20-23).
    * Sixth Paragraph: (1:24-31).
    * Seventh Paragraph: (2:1-3).

8. Each of the three nouns that occur in the first verse – are repeated in a given number of times that is a multiple of seven:

9. *God*: _____

10. *Heavens*: _____

11. *Earth*: _____

12. Ten sayings (Aboth v 1; in B. Rosh Hashana 32a).

13. These ten sayings are divided into two groups:

    Seven sayings regarding the creation of the creatures:

    ·   Let there be _____ (1:3)
    ·   Let there be _____ (1:6)

- Let the _____(1:9)
- Let the _____(1:12)
- Let there be _____(1:14)
- Let the _____ (1:20)
- Let the _____ (1:24)

The second group emphasizes God's concern for man's welfare:

- Let us make [not a command but an expression of the will to create man]_____
  _____(1:26)
- Be _____
  (1:28)
- Behold _____
  (1:29)

14. The terms *light* and *day* are found _____
    _____(2-5).

15. *Water* is mentioned_____(6-13)

16. *It was good* (the seventh time - *very good*).

17. The first verse has seven words: (את הארץ השמים
    בראשית ברא אלהים את) "*Barasheet bara Elohim et
    hashamaim v'et haeretz"[In the Beginning God
    created the heavens and the earth]*.

These first seven words, in Hebrew, comprise a total of twenty-eight letters, or, four times seven.

18. The second verse contains fourteen words – twice seven.

19. To suppose that all this is a mere coincidence is not possible.

20. That Moses wrote the first five books (Torah) is confirmed in Scripture: (Exod. 17:14; Lev. 1:1,2; Num. 33:2; Deut. 1:1; Josh. 1:7; 1 Kings 2:3; 2 Kings 14:6; Ezra 6:18; Neh. 13:1; Dan. 9:11-13; Mal. 4:4; Matt. 8:4; Mark 12:26; Luke 16:29; John 7:19; Acts 26:22; Rom. 10:19; 1 Cor. 9:9; 2 Cor. 3:15).

C. Purpose of Genesis

1. The purpose of the Torah_____ (Psa. 111:6):

2. Torah is a book of_____

3. When man failed _____

4. The patience and love of God is _____ _____

5. Personal growth, love, hate, pain, joy, tragedy, family, and hope.

FIRST WORDS: GENESIS 1:1-3

A. First Words (1:1)

1. The seven words *"Bereishit bara Elohim et hashamaim v'et haeretz* _____

   _____

2. The first word *bereishit* _____

   _____

3. It refers to the first phase _____

   _____

4. The statement of John 1:1 _____

   _____

5. The Messiah, the Logos, the Word, the Memra, preceded the creation of the heavens and the earth.

6. The first word of the Bible, (*bereishit*, "In the beginning") can be separated to form two words: (*bar/ber*) and (*asheet/eishit*).

7. The word (*bar*) means _____

   _____

8.   This word first appears in the Bible in Psalms 2:12 _____

9.   The second word (*asheet*) is a verb which means

    _____

    _____(Genesis 3:15)

10. "A Son I shall put/place/appoint."

11. A better rendering might be _____

    _____

12. The introduction of only a slight separation between the second and third letters of the Bible provides us with this insight.

13. Maybe Paul had this in mind when he encouraged Timothy in "correctly cutting the word."

14. The second word *bara* is _____

    _____

15. Create out of nothing, or create out of something.

16. When something is created, what is produced is new, fresh, and good.

17. Shaping, forming, and transforming.

18. *Bara* is used in the creation of the heavens and earth, 1:1; Jehovah created the heavens, Isa. 42:5; created the host of Heaven, Isa. 40:26; Creator of the ends of the earth, Isa. 40:28; created the north and the south, Psa. 89:12.

19. Of the creation of living creatures – of animal life, 1:21; of human life, 1:27 5:1,2; 6:7, Deut. 4:32; Psa. 89:47; Isa. 45:12; of the cosmic forces of nature, Isa. 45:7; Amos 4:13; of Israel, Eccl. 12:1; Isa. 43:1; Isa. 43:7; Isa. 43:15; Mal. 2:10.

20. Of transformation and renewal of things – God creates a new thing in the earth, Num. 16:30; He creates a clean heart, Psa. 51:10; He creates waters in the desert, Isa. 41:18-20; He creates salvation, Isa. 45:8; He creates peace, Isa. 57:19; the heavens and the earth, Isa. 65:17; Jerusalem, Isa. 65:18; a new thing, a woman shall encompass a man, Jer. 31:22.

21. *Ex nihilo*, "out of nothing" (Romans 4:17).

22. Verse one refers _____

_____

23. Chronologically precedes Genesis 1:1_____

_____

24. By means of this *Word*, the heavens and the earth were created (John 1:3). So both Genesis 1:1 and John 1:1 mention _____

_____

25. The *Messiah*, the *Logos*, the *Word*, the *Memra*, preceded the creation of the heavens and the earth.

26. *Memra*: _____

_____

27. Aramaic paraphrases of the Torah (*targums*)

_____

28. How can an infinite God fit in the finite universe?

29. Theological abstraction _____

_____

30. Projection of the infinite _____

_____

31. The Aramaic term is *Memra* (מימרא)

   *From the beginning, with wisdom the Word (מימרא,
   Memra) of the LORD created and perfected the
   heavens and the earth...And the Word of the
   LORD said: "Let there be light"; and there was
   light by his Word. (Genesis 1:1-3 Targum Neofati
   Yerushalmi).*

32. The *targum* depicts the *Memra* as _____

_____

33. In the gospel of John, the *Memra* of God seems
    to be equivalent to the *Logos* _____

_____

34. God sent forth His *Memra* to intersect the finite
    and to be clothed in garments of human flesh
    (John 1:14). So Miriam (Mary), a daughter of the
    house of Israel, "was found to be with child by
    the Holy Spirit" (Matt. 1:18).

B. Regarding Regrets

O God, You Who are the truth, make me one with You in love everlasting. I am often wearied by the many things I hear and read, but in You is all that I long for. Let the learned be still, let all creatures be silent before You; You alone speak to me. – The Doctrine of Truth, The Imitation of Christ. Thomas A Kempis

1. Every time the scripture is read Jews believe

_____

2. It is so when we read God's word, we seek

_____
_____(SOS 1:4)

Divine Origin

1. Every word and every letter comes from _____.

2. Looking at the very first word of scripture we get a sound bite of God's provision and purpose for His pinnacle of Creation – people.

For the Sake of Torah and Israel

1. The first word is בראשית (*bereishit*, in the beginning, Genesis 1:1) is really two words. Rashi, a revered rabbinical scholar (1040-1145 AD) stated, the two words, Bar & Reishit (rasheet), means "for the sake of Torah/Israel. *Bar* means "son" and *Reishit* means "I will put" (Gen. 3:15). Jewish scholars say that the "son" refers to Israel. Rashi

added the idea "for the sake of Torah" – Torah referring specifically to the 5 books of Moses, generally referring to all of scripture, or the Word (of God).

A Son I Will Put

1.   Simply, you can interpret *b'reishit* to mean "A Son (Bar) I will put (Rasheet)." Therefore, from the very beginning we have a reference to God's Son, an Anointed One that God will place, or appoint, or put. The Apostle John said it this way, "In the beginning was the Word, and the Word was with God, and the Word was God" (John 1:1).

2.   Jesus is the Torah/Word_____
    _____(John 1:14).

Facing Forward

1.   The first letter of the first word is ב (the Hebrew letter "bet").

2.   *Bet* is the second letter of the Hebrew alphabet.

3.   Are we to forget the past? (Psa. 77:11, 12)

Regarding Regrets

1. However, regarding regrets (Isa. 43:18, 19) _____
    _____
    _____

2. Here God says He will <u>make a way for you</u> and
    <u>sustain you</u>.

3. The first letter and the first word of the first book
    of scripture reminds us (Isaiah 41:10)

C. Spirit of God (1:2)

1. A young Jewish carpenter _____
    (Lk. 4:18).

2. He looked at those in attendance that day and
    said, 'Today this Scripture has been fulfilled in
    your hearing.' Doing this, He _____
    _____
    _____

3. What was this Spirit? Isaiah 11:1-2 "the Branch"
    (*Netzer* נצר) – which is a title for _____
    _____

    It is written, "He shall be called a Netzrin (Matt.
    2:23).

4. Isaiah is telling us that the Messiah will come
    _____

5.   In the Midrash Rabbah (6th Century CE) states that this Spirit of the Lord that is spoken of in Isaiah that is resting upon the Messiah is the same Spirit of the Lord that moved over the primeval waters of Creation:

"The Spirit of God was moving over the surface of the waters." This was the spirit of Messiah as it is written, "The Spirit of the Lord will rest on him (Genesis Rabbah 1:2)."

6.   To put Genesis in context we must go _____
     _____

7.   The opening verses of Moses is a _____
     _____

8.   Moses opens the account with the Axiom, "In the beginning God created."

9.   The declaration ends in Genesis 2:4 _____
     _____

D. Shekinah (1:3)

1.   One of the divine activities _____
     (Genesis 1:3-5; 14-16).

2.   What was this light that existed before the sun, moon and the stars?

3.   This essence of the Shekinah was manifested in
     _____

4. At the "end of time" the Shekinah will be present with the New Heaven and Earth (Revelation 22:5).

5. We have glimpses _____
    _____

6. We have a declaration _____
    _____

7. Light plays such an important role _____
    _____

8. An eternal light of divine origin _____
    _____

9. This 'holy lamp bore light in the Temple and from there to the world'.

10. The 'light' was set aside _____
    _____

11. Beautiful symbols (2 Corinthians 3:15) _____
    _____

12. 'Light' is synonymous _____
    _____

13. Angelic announcement (Luke 2:9).

14. Joseph and Mary entered the Temple (Luke 2:32).

15. Jesus (John 8:12) _____
    _____

16. 'Darkness' _____
   _____

17. Tradition, religion, self-esteem and self-awareness
   (Psalm 119:105) _____

18. Apostle John (John 1:1,14) _____

19. Jesus, 'Passover Lamb,' (Hebrews 9:22) _____
   _____

20. 'The true Light', (John 1:9).

21. The reason some (both Jew and Gentile) do not come to the light is simply, as Augustine (354-430) stated in his first homily on the Gospel of John:

   'There are insensitive hearts, still incapable of receiving this Light because the weight of their sins prevents them from seeing it. Let them not imagine that the Light is absent because they do not see it, for on account of their sins they are in darkness.' 'And the light shineth in darkness; and the darkness comprehended it not' (John 1:5). 'Therefore, like the blind man exposed to the sun, the sun being present to him but he being absent from the sun, so the insensitive one, the sinner, the impious has a blind heart'.

22. Examine _____
   _____
   _____

23. 'Ye are the light (Matthew 5:14-16).

24. Fundamental pillars _____
    _____

25. God is there _____
    _____

26. He is the pre-existent God _____
    _____

27. "For He spoke and it was done" (Psalm 33:9).

28. Creation the second letter "bet" or "b," - Ten
    Commandments opens with, "I am the Lord your
    God," or the Hebrew word *anokhi,* thus beginning
    with the first Hebrew letter, "alef," or "a."

29. "Creation is secondary _____
    _____

30. New Testament (2 Timothy 2:15; 3:16; John 1).

31. The Midrash takes the word for "beginning"
    (*reishit*) as a synonym for "Torah" (Prov. 8:22),
    interpreting the first verse as declaring: "With
    reishit did God create the heaven and the earth."
    God created the world by consulting the Torah,
    fashioning a world based on Torah values, for
    the sake of the Torah, so that there would be
    somewhere in the universe where the values of
    the Torah could be put into practice (Genesis
    Rabbah 1:1, 6).

32. Truth (אמת)

God has a plan for humanity. It involves
understanding truth. The Hebrew word translated
truth, is *emet (John 14:6).*

33. Torah Fulfilled

According to the ancients, even the name of
Messiah spelled backwards spells the name *Ha
Shem*, meaning "there will then live, the name of
the Almighty"

34. Genesis points us to the Word _____

_____

35. (Matthew 5:17; John 16:33) _____

_____

CHAPTER TWO

THE SEVEN DAYS: GENESIS 1:2 – 2:3

A. The First Paragraph: The First Day 1:3-5

1. Verse 2 serves as an introduction to the six days of Creation. It shows the seven steps of God's creative work:

2. *And God said* _____

3. *Let there be* _____

4. *And there was* is the fulfillment _____

   _____

5. *And God made* is the action _____

   _____

6. *And God called,* or *And God blessed* – is the act of _____

7. *And God saw that it was good* – is God's evaluation, expressing _____

8. *And it was evening and it was morning of day* – is the _____

9. Verse 2 also created a problem that was remedied by the six-days of creation. *Tohu*, means _____

_____

10. The word <u>was</u> can be translated _____

_____

- Support for this view is seen in Isaiah 45:18.
- Lucifer's fall (Isaiah 14:12-17; Ezek. 28:11-19).

11. Paul makes an interesting use of the creation story (2 Cor. 4:6).

12. We can see in Genesis 1 a picture of _____

_____

13. Verse 2 created a problem, *Tohu*, means "without form," emphasizing formlessness, was rectified in the first three days. The first three days are days of division, or opposites.

   ·   First day: _____

           _____

   ·   Second day: _____

           _____

   ·   Third day: _____

           _____

14. *Vohu,* meaning "empty" or "emptiness," was remedied in the second three days, or the days of decoration.

· On the fourth day _____

· On the fifth day _____

· On the sixth day _____

15. The above suggests in this first chapter of Genesis you find parallelism and symmetry. All things came into being at God's Word. Psalm 33:3-9 affirms such.

B. The Second Paragraph: The Second Day 1:6-8

1. Verse 5 *"the day of the One."*

2. "God-divided rather than sun-divided _____
   _____"

3. The *"firmament"* or expanse is referring to the atmosphere that encircles our planet.

   Sky" or heaven in Hebrew: *shamayim.* The Midrash (Gen. R. 4:7) understands the word as a combination of *esh* (fire) and *mayim* (water), that is, the sun and the rain clouds.

4. Were the rain clouds to extinguish the sun or were the sun to evaporate the rain clouds, the word would perish.

5. Therefore, God works a daily miracle. Fire and water agree to co-exist peacefully so that the world can endure. Another midrash (Deut. R. 1:12)

links this idea to a passage in Jewish prayers:

"May you who establish peace in the heavens [teaching fire and water to get along] grant that kind of peace to us and to all the people Israel"

6. On the second day we miss the formula "and God saw that it was good" (Rashi).

7. Genesis 1:7 describes the result of 1:6 _____

8. The verse ends the phrase: *and it was so.* The Hebrew word here is *ken.*

   Job 37:18, He *spread out the sky [like] a molten mirror.*

   Isaiah 40:22, He *stretches out the heavens as a curtain, and spreads them out as a tent to dwell in.*

C. Third Paragraph: The Third Day 1:9-13

1. On the third day, two works were done.

2. Verse 9 states: *gathered into one place* _____

3. In 1:10a is the naming, regarding the seas – The Hebrew reads: *mikveh hamayim,* meaning that the waters were gathered into reservoirs (or pool – like a mikveh) *called...Seas* – this is the last

thing God names in the creation account.

4.   Verse 10b gives the result.

5.   In 1:11-12 we find the second work.

6.   There are three divisions of the vegetable kingdom, all related to the Hebrew commandment: *Let the earth put forth, or sprout.*

The first term is *deshe eisev*, a general term that includes grass and grain – the word literally means _____

The second category is *mazria zera*, literally meaning "seeding seed _____

_____

The third category is *eitz pri*, which refers to

_____

The species are now self-perpetuating – the result was: *and it was so.*

7.   In verse 12 *God saw* _____

_____

D. Fourth Paragraph: The Fourth Day 1:14-19

1.   The purpose _____

_____

_____

_____

2.   This is the fourth division _____
     _____

3.   The primordial light _____
     _____

4.   God hid the primordial light (Messianic Light) until such time as humans would be able to stand it, replacing it with the light of the sun (BT Hagigah 12a)

5.   The purpose of the lights include:

     First: (Job 38:31; Psa. 19:1; Jer. 31:35, 36)
     _____

     Second: *moadim* _____
     _____

     Third: _____
     _____

     Fourth: _____
     _____

     Fifth: _____
     _____

6.   Verses 16 – 18 expand upon the results of verses 14 & 15 – Greater & Lesser Lights.

7.   Sun & Moon _____
     _____

8. In this sense, Jews pray at a *bris millah* "May this small one become great" – for a growing child is the recipient of wisdom and training from parents and teachers. They pray that the infant will grow up to become an independent source of greatness, who will enlighten others.

9. *He made the stars also (16)* _____
    _____

10. Fifty chapters about the Tabernacle, five words about the stars.

    The Bible is a handbook _____
    _____

11. *God* (Hebrew, *"Elohim,"* making reference to His majestic power).

12. The phrase, *"He made the stars also,"* is like an after- thought, *"Oh, by the way, God* (Elohim) *created the stars also."*

13. (Isaiah 42:5, 6) _____
    _____

14. (Psalm 8:4, 5; Ephesians 2:7) _____
    _____

15. (Psalm 40:17; Acts 17:28; Hebrews 13:5; Colossians 2:10; 3:11)

    Therefore, rest in the confidence that He who

"made the stars also" can complete that which He has started in you and will hold your hand; and keep you along the journey.

The end result of the fourth day – *God saw that it was good.*

E. Fifth Paragraph: The Fifth Day 1:20-23

1. The purpose _____
    _____

    The Hebrew says *yishretzu sheretz* _____
    _____

2. God created (Heb. *bara*) _____
    _____

3. Sea monsters: the Hebrew word is *tannin* and the word "Leviathan."

4. Then God blessed them to multiply.

5. (*Praise the Lord from the earth, Sea monsters and all deeps, Psa. 148:7*). The rabbis declare that the sea creatures and birds needed a special blessing because many of them would be caught and destroyed.

6. Man's domain _____
    _____

7. Fish and fowl have much in common.

8.   Water is preeminently the seat of life.

9.   There is no such thing as bigness or smallness to a God who is infinite.

F. Sixth Paragraph: The Sixth Day 1:24-31

1.   God made His final preparation of the earth as man's domain. He made three categories of land animals:

First: _____

_____

Second: _____

_____

Third: _____

_____

The conclusion was *and God saw that it was good.*

2.   Scientists have classified millions of different species of animals, including more than 800,000 different kinds of insects, 30,000 kinds of fish, 9,000 kinds of birds, 6,000 kinds of reptiles, 3,000 kinds of amphibians, and 5,000 kinds of mammals.

3.   Where did all this bewildering variety of life form come from?

4. If Genesis 1 were a psalm, it would have doubtless concluded with a resounding "Selah" – There. What do you think of that!

5. Creation of human beings – a combination of the heavens and the earthy, the sublime and the physical

6. The three words, *Let us make* _____
    _____

7. The use of the plural pronoun *Let us* _____
    _____

8. The rabbis teach that God was speaking to angels – however the text never indicates angels were part of the conversation.

9. If God had consulted, it would have said so as in the case of 1 Kings 22:19-23, where God consulted with the heavenly court about doing something.

10. In our image, in Hebrew is one word *betzalmeinu*. The root is *tzalam*, and refers to the original image or imitation. This same word is also used of idols.

11. In the ancient Near East, the ruling king was often described as the "image" or the "likeness" of a god which served to elevate the monarch above ordinary mortals.

12. In the Bible, this idea became _____

_____

13. This preamble (*Let us make man*) indicates

_____

14. In our image, or in Our mold (Rashi) _____

_____

15. *According (after) our likeness* is one Hebrew word *kidmuteinu* which means "a model" or "a copy" (Psa. 8:3-5).

16. Man is in no way related to the beasts.

    Even the most primitive human tribe possesses linguistics of a subtle, complex and eloquent nature. Man stands alone.

17. *Physically; mentally; spiritually* _____

_____

18. Man, *Adam* _____

_____

19. God created man – He created him – He created them (27).

    ·   Man's creation

    ·   Created in _____

    _____

    ·   Both man and woman were created on ____

    _____

20. Genesis 1:28-30 presents the Edenic Covenant, which is the first of eight covenants of the Bible. (*Edenic Covenant*, Gen. 1:28-30; 2:15-17; *Adamic Covenant*, Gen. 3:14-19; *Noahic Covenant*, Gen. 8:20-9:170; *Abrahamic Covenant*, Gen. 12:1-3; *Mosaic Covenant*, Exod. 20-23; Deuteronomy; *Davidic Covenant*, 2 Sam. 7:4-17; *Land Covenant*, Deut. 30:1-10; *New Covenant*, Jer. 31:31-37.

21. The Edenic Covenant spelled out in two parts:

The first part, (1:28-30), begins _____
_____

This covenant is made between God and _____
_____
(Hosea 6:7 refers to this).

The second part, (vv. 28b – 30) list four specific provisions of the Edenic covenant.

Provision one: Populate the earth.

Provision two: Subdue _____

Provision three: Rule over _____

Provision four: Diet _____

22. In verse 31 *very good.*

23. *The sixth day*: For the first time, there is the use of the definite article.

24. This is the second time that uniqueness is emphasized _____
_____

G. Seventh Paragraph: The Seventh Day 2:1-3

1. Five things: _____
_____

2. Genesis 2:2 no longer creation, but procreation.

3. The creation was complete.

4. The Hebrew word for rested is *shabbat*, which means _____

5. *Shabbat* here is a verb, not a noun.

6. Ten times in verses 2 and 3 God is mentioned The Edenic Covenant contained no commandment to Adam and Eve to keep _____

7. The word *sanctified* or *hallowed* means _____
_____

    Therefore, God ceased His creative work on that day from that which He *created (bara)* and from that which He had *made (asah).*

8. Later in Israel's history, God's resting on the seventh day becomes the basis _____
_____
_____
_____

9. Some observations of this section (Gen.2:1-3)

   First: The Hebrew text has _____

   _____

   Second: Verses 2 through 3a contain three _____

   _____

   Third: The exact middle expression is the _____

   _____

   Fourth: The three middle clauses (2a, 2b, 3a) ____

   _____

   Fifth: The phrase, "his work," is found _____

   _____

10. New Testament quotations and applications of Genesis 1:1 – 2:3.

11. Sabbath – double portion of manna given on Friday (Exodus 16:4).

12. Today we rest, not on a special day but in a Person.

   So there remains a Sabbath rest for the people of God. For the one who has entered His rest has himself also rested from his works, as God did from His. Therefore, let us be diligent to enter that rest (Hebrews 4:9-11a).

   Come to Me all who are weary and heavy-laden, and I will give you rest (Matt. 11:28).

CHAPTER THREE

HISTORY (*TOLDOT*) OF THE HEAVENS AND EARTH GENESIS 2:4 – 2:7

A. Introduction to the History 2:4

1. The Lord God – This is the unspoken, unique, holy, personal divine name YHVH (יהוה) of God. Elohim (אלהים), the general term of God, is used many times, YHVH is used here in verse four and again in the Torah found in Exodus 9:30.

2. The first *toldot* is sometimes called "The Tablet of _____." As earlier stated, the *toldot* tells us "what became of," in this case what became of *the heavens and of the earth* that God had *created*. Whereas in the creation account, God blessed three times; now in this *toldot*, He will _____ three times.

3. Genesis 2:4 states: *in the day*. Here the Hebrew word is *yom* is used without a numeral, and without a numeral it can refer to a longer _____.

4.   The theology of this section teaches several things.

First: _____
_____

Second: _____
_____

Third: _____
_____

Fourth: this section emphasizes man over creation
in general, and so it gives us details on the
creation of man and details on man's nature
as God's image.

Fifth: _____
_____

Sixth: _____
_____

5.   The Name יהוה (YHVH) also signifies the eternity
of God, because its letters are also those of the
words:

היה – (HYH) _____

הוה –(HVH) _____

ויהיה –(VYHYH)_____

6.   The Four-letter Name is often translated the
Eternal One. This is also the proper Name of
God. In respect for its intense holiness, it is

not pronounced as it is spelled. In prayer or when reciting a complete Scriptural verse, it is pronounced Adonai. Otherwise, it is referred to as HASHEM, or the Name.

7. *These are the "toldot" (generations, history, account) of the heavens and the earth when they were created.*

The *Midrash Rabbah* contains an unusual Messianic interpretation that is worth retelling simply for the sake of its novelty.

In *Genesis Rabbah* 12:6, the Sages point out that the word "generations" (toldot, תולדות) in Genesis 2:4 is spelled with two *vavim* (ו). In all other instances, except for one in the book of Ruth, the word is spelled with only one *vav* (תולדת).

8. Since the sages assumed that every letter of Torah is significant (even Yeshua taught that every jot and tittle is eternal), they searched tiny discrepancies like this for meaning.

In this case, they explain that prior to Adam's sin, the word "generations" (toldot) was spelled with two *vavim* (תולדות) to indicate that the generations of Adam and the generations of all creation were

---

9. But subsequent to sin, those generations were diminished. Their diminution is indicated by the defective spelling of the word of toldot (תולדת). Adam's sin affected even the heavens and the earth.

Rabbi Berekiah said in the name of Rabbi Shmuel bar Nachman, "Though these things were created in their fullness, yet when Adam sinned they were spoiled, and they will not be restored to their fullness until the Son of Perez [i.e. the Messiah] comes, as it says [in Ruth 4:18], "Now these are the generations (toldot, תולדות) of Perez." (Genesis Rabbah 12:6)

10. Rabbi Berekiah sees a Messianic meaning in this restored spelling. Messiah is the one who will restore both the generations of mankind and the generations of the whole creation. He calls Messiah the "Son of Perez" because in Ruth 4:18, *Perez* stands at the head of David's genealogy – the *toldot* of the Davidic monarchy from which _____(Romans 8:20-22).

B. Creation of Man 2:5-7

1. **Vs. 5:** *[HASHEM]* God had not sent rain because there was no man to work the soil. But when Adam was created, he recognized its importance for the world.

   He prayed, and rain fell, causing the trees and vegetation to spring forth (Rashi).

   As noted [previously] plant life had already been created and was waiting just below the surface for Adam to pray – The Talmudic sage Rav Assi noted the apparent contradiction between 1:12 (earth brought forth vegetation) & 2:5 (that nothing had grown prior to the creation of Adam) [was] that the herbs began to grow on the third day, as they had been commanded, but stopped before they broke through the soil. It remained for Adam to pray for them, whereupon rain fell, and the growth was completed. This teaches that_____ (Chullin 60b).

2. This demonstrates a basic article of faith (within Judaism): God provides what Man needs, but it is up to Man to pray and otherwise carry out his

_____

_____

3. *No shrub in the field* describes the initial state of _____after dry land appeared as recorded in Gen. 1:9-10.

    Rain is not only a natural phenomenon it is also a

    _____

4. *No man to cultivate the ground* – Agriculture is regarded _____

    _____

5. **Vs. 6:** God caused the deep (subterranean waters) to rise, (moistening the dry earth), forming low-flying clouds filled with water to moisten the dust (arid earth), from which Adam _____

    _____

6. **Vs. 7:** *Dust* is a word that can be used synonymously with "clay." The verb "formed" (va-yitzer) is often used in the Bible to describe the activity of a _____ (yotzer).

7. *Yitzer* (formed) is used here, whereas, in Chapter one, *Bara* (created) was used. *Bara* emphasizes something only God can do – that is create something out of nothing. *Yitzer* (formed) emphasizes _____

_____

_____

Yitzer is used of a potter shaping clay (Isa. 29:16, Jer. 18:1-17); goldsmiths who make idols (Isa. 44:9, Hab. 2:18); regarding the shaping of Messiah's body in the womb (Isa. 49:5); also, where God forms hearts (Psa. 33:15); the eye (Psa. 94:9); and when God formed man (Psa. 119:73).

8. Genesis 2:7 the word *yitzer* is written with two *yods* (יי), וייצר. In 2:19, it is written properly with one *yod* (י), ויצר. Rabbis suggest a few explanations for the inconsistency regarding spelling: first, the two yods represent the two inclinations: the good inclination and the evil inclination; second, or it refers to the creation of both the material and the immaterial; third, or it refers to a double forming, one for this world, and one for the resurrection. This symbol is evocative of the notion of God's

_____

_____(Isa. 29:16; 45:9).

9. Man's "glory and freedom" is dependent upon God. Human sovereignty can never quite be absolute. It must always be_____

    _____

10. J.I. Packer states, "What were we made for? To know God. What aim should we set ourselves in life? To know God. What is the 'eternal life' that Jesus gives? _____
    _____(Jeremiah 9:23,24; Hosea 6:6).

11. One scholar makes this observation of the Hebrew word "life" (Chaim or Hayyim or HYYM, no vowels in Hebrew, simply vowel sounds). We are granted not one life _____

    _____

12. For life, to be true life, it cannot be lived alone. This speaks of the need for _____

    _____

    _____

13. Central to the word (HaYYiM, חיים), the Hebrew word for life, are two yods (YY, יי), which combined form _____

    _____

14. Belief in the Almighty replaces the great 'if' of life. When God is central to our lives, doubt and despair are replaced by confidence and divine comfort – God is the _____

    _____

    _____

15. *Man...Ground* – In Hebrew is *Adam* (אדם) &
    Adamah (אדמה) a word play emphasizing man's

---

16. *The Breath of Life* – Genesis 2:7b deals with
    the immaterial part of man. In Hebrew it is
    nishmat chaim (נשמת חיים). This is the *neshamah*,
    or   the_____;   and
    the word is used twenty-five times in the Old
    Testament.

17. God's breath brings animation, causing man to
    become a *living soul*. In Job 32:8, it also brings
    spiritual understanding. Therefore, the result is

---

18. The Hebrew word *ruach* (spirit, wind) is used of
    God, man, animal, and idols, the word *neshamah*
    is used only of God and man, except once, where
    it is used of animals in Genesis 7:22.

19. It is this breath of God, the *neshamah*, that produced
    the _____ (Job
    34:14-15; Psa. 104:29; Isa. 2:22).

20. The *neshamah* is also found in animals (Gen.
    7:22), but only to man _____

---

21. This means that not only is man physical, man
    is also_____. The result of this
    "breathing in" was; and man became a living
    soul. The living soul in Hebrew is *nephesh*

chayah. This concept of living soul is also found in animals (Gen. 1:24, 30; 2:19), but, like the spirit, the soul of man is far more complex and eternal than the animal.

22. First Corinthians 15:45 mentions that the first man, Adam, was made a living soul, and this is based upon this particular passage. Therefore, man's uniqueness does not lie in the fact of the *breath of life* as such, because the same words are used of the animal kingdom. However, man's uniqueness lies in the fact that he has the _____, and the animal kingdom does not.

23. And He blew into his nostrils the soul of life. God thus made Man out of both lower (earthly) and upper (heavenly) matter: his body from the dust and his soul from the spirit (Rashi).

The Jewish sages state, *"one who blows, blows from within himself,"* indicating that Man's soul is part of God's_____, as it were.

24. *Soul* derives from the Hebrew root *"Nephesh"* which has several connotations:

- *Breath, or the Principle of Life*: When t h i s breath is absent there is death. At death the
  _____

- *Mind and Rationality*: The idea is that the soul not only discovers the trustworthy but persuades _____ _____to place his trust in it or cast his all upon it.

- *The seat of Affections, Feelings and Emotions*:

    The soul, which the Lord breathed into the body, feels after the Lord and upon discovering Him is moved to_____

    _____

- *It Signifies a Person*: That which can love or hate; that which can sing or be sad; that which can be excited by the right or by the wrong makes up the_____

    _____

25. The soul, the breath of God, came from God and through faith in Jesus Christ it returns to spend eternity with its _____

    _____

    You are different from the beasts of the field by virtue of your "intellect, free will, self-awareness, consciousness of the existence of others, conscience, responsibility and _____

    _____
    _____

    Being created 'in the image of God' implies that human life is infinitely _____

    _____

    David exclaimed, "I am fearfully and wonderfully made" (Psalm 139:14).

Bibliography:

Blech, Benjamin, *More Secrets of Hebrew Words*, Northvale, NY, Jason Aronson, (1993).

Blech, Benjamin, *Secrets of Hebrew Words*, Northvale, NY, Jason Aronson, (1991).

Clark, Mary, Augustine of Hippo - *Selected Writings*, New York, NY, Paulist Press, (1984).

Cassuto, U., *A Commentary on the book of Genesis, Part 1 From Adam to Noah, Genesis I – VI 8*, Jerusalem, The Magnes Press, The Hebrew University, (1978).

Fruchtenbaum, Arnold G., *The Book of Genesis, Ariel's Bible Commentary*, San Antonio, TX, Ariel Ministries, (2009).

Johnson, Jeffrey D., *He Made the Stars Also, Messianic Reflections*, Eugene, OR, Wipf and Stock Publishers, (2003).

Johnson, Jeffrey D., *God Was There, Genesis Chapters 1-12*, Eugene, OR, Wipf and Stock Publishers, (2005).

Lancaster, D.T., *Commentary on the Life and Times of the Messiah from a Hebraic Perspective, Volume Four*, B'sorat HaMashiach, The Good News of Messiah, Marshfield, MO., First Fruits of Zion, (2002).

Lancaster, D.T., *Messianic Commentary on the Parashot HaShavuah, Volume Two, Shadows of the Messiah*, Littleton, CO., First Fruits of Zion, (2006).

Lash, Jamie, *A Kiss A Day*, Hagerstown, MD, Ebed Publications, (1996)

Lieber, David L., Etz Hayim, *Torah and Commentary*, New York, NY, The Jewish Publication Society, (1999), The Rabbinical Assembly (2001).

Novak, Al, *Hebrew Honey*, Houston, C&D International, (1987)

Packer, J.I., *Knowing God*, Downers Grove, IL., Inter Varsity Press, (1973)

Phillips, John, *Exploring Genesis*, Neptune, New Jersey, Loizeaux Brothers, (1980)

Rotherham, Joseph Bryant, *Rotherham's Emphasized Bible*, Grand Rapids, MI, Kregel Pulications, 1994

Sarna, Nahum M., *Understanding Genesis, The Heritage of Biblical Israel*, New York, Schocken Books, 1970

Scherman, Nosson, *The Chumash, The Torah: Haftaros and Five Megillos with a Commentary Anthologized from the Rabbinic Writings*, Brooklyn, NY, Mesorah Publication, Ltd., (2000).

Trepp, Leo, *A History Of The Jewish Experience, Eternal Faith, Eternal People*, New York, NY, Behrman House, Inc., (1973).

ENDNOTES

1   Lash, Jamie, *A Kiss A Day*, Hagerstown, MD, Ebed Publications, (1996), p. 17.

2   Fruchtenbaum, Arnold G., *The Book of Genesis, Ariel's Bible Commentary,* San Antonio, TX, Ariel Ministries, (2009), p. 1.

3   Ibid.

4   Cassuto, U., *A Commentary on the book of Genesis, Part 1 From Adam to Noah, Genesis I – VI 8*, Jerusalem, The Magnes Press, The Hebrew University, (1978), p. 13.

5   Ibid., pp. 14, 15.

6   Fruchtenbaum, Arnold G., *The Book of Genesis, Ariel's Bible Commentary*, San Antonio, TX, Ariel Ministries, (2009), p. 5.

7   Fruchtenbaum, Arnold G., *The Book of Genesis, Ariel's Bible Commentary,* San Antonio, TX, Ariel Ministries, (2009), pp. 30, 31.

8   Ibid., pp. 31, 32

9   Ibid., pp. 30, 31

10   Lancaster, D.T., *Messianic Commentary on the Parashot HaShavuah, Volume Two, Shadows of the Messiah,* Littleton, CO., First Fruits of Zion, (2006), p. 4.

11   Ibid., p. 3.

12   Johnson, Jeffrey D., *God Was There, Genesis Chapters 1-12*, Eugene, OR, Wipf and Stock Publishers, (2005), pp. 1, 2.

13   Trepp, Leo, *A History Of The Jewish Experience, Eternal Faith, Eternal People*, New York, NY, Behrman House, Inc., (1973), p. 203.

14   Blech, Benjamin, *More Secrets of Hebrew Words*, Northvale, NY, Jason Aronson, (1993), p. 17.

15   Blech, Benjamin, *Secrets of Hebrew Words*, Northvale, NY, Jason Aronson, (1991), p. 30.

16   Clark, Mary, *Augustine of Hippo - Selected Writings*, New York, NY, Paulist Press, (1984), p. 280.

17   Johnson, Jeffrey D., *God Was There, Genesis Chapters 1-12*, Eugene, OR, Wipf and Stock Publishers, (2005), p. 26.

18   Blech, Benjamin, *Secrets of Hebrew Words*, Northvale, NY, Jason Aronson, (1991), p. 33.

19   Lieber, David L., *Etz Hayim, Torah and Commentary,* New York, NY, The Jewish Publication Society, (1999), The Rabbinical Assembly (2001), p. 3.

20   Blech, Benjamin, *Secrets of Hebrew Words*, Northvale, NY, Jason Aronson, (1991), p. 191.

21   Phillips, John, *Exploring Genesis*, Neptune, New Jersey, Loizeaux Brothers, (1980), pp. 39, 40.

22   Fruchtenbaum, Arnold G., *The Book of Genesis, Ariel's Bible Commentary,* San Antonio, TX, Ariel Ministries, (2009), pp. 42, 43.

23 Lieber, David L., *Etz Hayim, Torah and Commentary,* New York, NY, The Jewish Publication Society, (1999), The Rabbinical Assembly (2001), pp. 5, 6.

24 Rotherham, Joseph Bryant, *Rotherham's Emphasized Bible,* Grand Rapids, MI, Kregel Pulications, 1994, p. 33.

25 Scherman, Nosson, *The Chumash, The Torah: Haftaros and Five Megillos with a Commentary Anthologized from the Rabbinic Writings,* Brooklyn, NY, Mesorah Publication, Ltd., (2000), p. 4.

26 Lieber, David L., *Etz Hayim, Torah and Commentary,* New York, NY, The Jewish Publication Society, (1999), The Rabbinical Assembly (2001), p. 6.

27 Fruchtenbaum, Arnold G., *The Book of Genesis, Ariel's Bible Commentary,* San Antonio, TX, Ariel Ministries, (2009), pp. 47, 48.

28 Ibid. pp. 49, 50, 51.

29 Ibid. p. 52.

30 Lieber, David L., *Etz Hayim, Torah and Commentary,* New York, NY, The Jewish Publication Society, (1999), The Rabbinical Assembly (2001), p. 7.

31 Fruchtenbaum, Arnold G., *The Book of Genesis, Ariel's Bible Commentary,* San Antonio, TX, Ariel Ministries, (2009), p. 51.

32 Scherman, Nosson, *The Chumash, The Torah: Haftaros and Five Megillos with a Commentary Anthologized from the Rabbinic Writings*, Brooklyn, NY, Mesorah Publication, Ltd., (2000), pp. 6, 7.

33 Phillips, John, *Exploring Genesis*, Neptune, New Jersey, Loizeaux Brothers, (1980), p. 43.

34 Johnson, Jeffrey D., *He Made the Stars Also, Messianic Reflections*, Eugene, OR, Wipf and Stock Publishers, (2003), pp. 19, 20.

35 Fruchtenbaum, Arnold G., *The Book of Genesis, Ariel's Bible Commentary,* San Antonio, TX, Ariel Ministries, (2009), p. 53.

36 Scherman, Nosson, *The Chumash, The Torah: Haftaros and Five Megillos with a Commentary Anthologized from the Rabbinic Writings*, Brooklyn, NY, Mesorah Publication, Ltd., (2000), p. 7.

37 Fruchtenbaum, Arnold G., *The Book of Genesis, Ariel's Bible Commentary,* San Antonio, TX, Ariel Ministries, (2009), p. 54.

38 Phillips, John, *Exploring Genesis*, Neptune, New Jersey, Loizeaux Brothers, (1980), p. 44.

39 Fruchtenbaum, Arnold G., *The Book of Genesis, Ariel's Bible Commentary,* San Antonio, TX, Ariel Ministries, (2009), p. 55.

40 Phillips, John, *Exploring Genesis*, Neptune, New Jersey, Loizeaux Brothers, (1980), pp. 44, 45.

41 Lieber, David L., *Etz Hayim, Torah and Commentary,* New York, NY, The Jewish Publication Society, (1999), The Rabbinical Assembly (2001), p. 9.

42 Fruchtenbaum, Arnold G., *The Book of Genesis, Ariel's Bible Commentary,* San Antonio, TX, Ariel Ministries, (2009), p. 56.

43 Ibid.

44 Lieber, David L., *Etz Hayim, Torah and Commentary,* New York, NY, The Jewish Publication Society, (1999), The Rabbinical Assembly (2001), p. 9.

45 Scherman, Nosson, *The Chumash, The Torah: Haftaros and Five Megillos with a Commentary Anthologized from the Rabbinic Writings,* Brooklyn, NY, Mesorah Publication, Ltd., (2000), p. 8.

46 Ibid., pp. 8, 9.

47 Phillips, John, *Exploring Genesis,* Neptune, New Jersey, Loizeaux Brothers, (1980), p. 45.

48 Fruchtenbaum, Arnold G., *The Book of Genesis, Ariel's Bible Commentary,* San Antonio, TX, Ariel Ministries, (2009), pp. 60, 61.

49 Ibid., p. 63

50 Phillips, John, *Exploring Genesis,* Neptune, New Jersey, Loizeaux Brothers, (1980), p. 47.

51 Fruchtenbaum, Arnold G., *The Book of Genesis, Ariel's Bible Commentary,* San Antonio, TX, Ariel Ministries, (2009), p. 63.

52 Phillips, John, *Exploring Genesis,* Neptune, New Jersey, Loizeaux Brothers, (1980), p. 47.

53 Fruchtenbaum, Arnold G., *The Book of Genesis, Ariel's Bible Commentary,* San Antonio, TX, Ariel Ministries, (2009), 63, 64.

54   Lieber, David L., *Etz Hayim, Torah and Commentary,* New York, NY, The Jewish Publication Society, (1999), The Rabbinical Assembly (2001), p. 12.

55   Fruchtenbaum, Arnold G., *The Book of Genesis, Ariel's Bible Commentary,* San Antonio, TX, Ariel Ministries, (2009), p. 64.

56   Ibid., p. 66.

57   Scherman, Nosson, *The Chumash, The Torah: Haftaros and Five Megillos with a Commentary Anthologized from the Rabbinic Writings,* Brooklyn, NY, Mesorah Publication, Ltd., (2000), p. 11.

58   Fruchtenbaum, Arnold G., *The Book of Genesis, Ariel's Bible Commentary,* San Antonio, TX, Ariel Ministries, (2009), p. 69.

59   Ibid.

60   Ibid., p. 70

61   Scherman, Nosson, *The Chumash, The Torah: Haftaros and Five Megillos with a Commentary Anthologized from the Rabbinic Writings,* Brooklyn, NY, Mesorah Publication, Ltd., (2000), p. 11.

62   Lancaster, D.T., *Messianic Commentary on the Parashot HaShavuah, Volume Two, Shadows of the Messiah,* Littleton, CO., First Fruits of Zion, (2006), pp. 7, 8.

63   Scherman, Nosson, *The Chumash, The Torah: Haftaros and Five Megillos with a Commentary Anthologized from the Rabbinic Writings,* Brooklyn, NY, Mesorah Publication, Ltd., (2000), pp. 5, 11.

64   Lieber, David L., *Etz Hayim, Torah and Commentary*, New York, NY, The Jewish Publication Society, (1999), The Rabbinical Assembly (2001), p. 13.

65   Scherman, Nosson, *The Chumash, The Torah: Haftaros and Five Megillos with a Commentary Anthologized from the Rabbinic Writings*, Brooklyn, NY, Mesorah Publication, Ltd., (2000), p. 11.

66   Lieber, David L., *Etz Hayim, Torah and Commentary*, New York, NY, The Jewish Publication Society, (1999), The Rabbinical Assembly (2001), p. 13.

67   Fruchtenbaum, Arnold G., *The Book of Genesis, Ariel's Bible Commentary*, San Antonio, TX, Ariel Ministries, (2009), pp. 72, 73.

68   Sarna, Nahum M., *Understanding Genesis, The Heritage of Biblical Israel*, New York, Schocken Books, 1970, p. 16.

69   Ibid.

70   Packer, J.I., *Knowing God*, Downers Grove, IL., Inter Varsity Press, (1973), p. 33.

71   Blech, Benjamin, *Secrets of Hebrew Words*, Northvale, NY, Jason Aronson, (1991), pp. 45, 46, 47.

72   Fruchtenbaum, Arnold G., *The Book of Genesis, Ariel's Bible Commentary*, San Antonio, TX, Ariel Ministries, (2009), p. 74.

73   Ibid., pp. 74, 75.

74   Lieber, David L., *Etz Hayim, Torah and Commentary,* New York, NY, The Jewish Publication Society, (1999), The Rabbinical Assembly (2001), p. 13.

75   Scherman, Nosson, *The Chumash, The Torah: Haftaros and Five Megillos with a Commentary Anthologized from the Rabbinic Writings,* Brooklyn, NY, Mesorah Publication, Ltd., (2000), p. 11.

76   Ibid.

77   Novak, Al, *Hebrew Honey,* Houston, C&D International, (1987), p. 242.

78   Blech, Benjamin, *Secrets of Hebrew Words,* Northvale, NY, Jason Aronson, (1991), p. 129.

79   Sarna, Nahum M., *Understanding Genesis, The Heritage of Biblical Israel,* New York, Schocken Books, 1970, p. 16.

80   Ibid.

www.ingramcontent.com/pod-product-compliance
Lightning Source LLC
LaVergne TN
LVHW051129080426
835510LV00018B/2317